TERRAFORMED

TERRAFORMED:

YOUNG BLACK LIVES IN THE INNER CITY

Joy White

Published by Repeater Books

An imprint of Watkins Media Ltd

Unit 11 Shepperton House

89-93 Shepperton Road

London

N1 3DF

United Kingdom

www.repeaterbooks.com

A Repeater Books paperback original 2020

2

Distributed in the United States by Random House, Inc., New York.

Copyright © Joy White 2020

Joy White asserts the moral right to be identified as the author of this work.

ISBN: 9781912248681

Ebook ISBN: 9781912248698

Printed and bound in the United Kingdom by TJ Books Ltd

CONTENTS

PROLOGUE: PRIVATE TROUBLES, PUBLIC CONCERNS

Newham is a London borough. It lies north of the river Thames, five miles to the east of the City of London. Over a two-year period from 2015 to 2016, I had many conversations with four young Newham residents who were born in 1991: Matt, Chris, Michael, and Amy. Some of the conversations were brief, some in depth and at length. In our talks we explored why it seemed that, no matter how hard they tried, the road to an independent adult life was just so difficult. I refer to them as the "Class of '91", using this as a shorthand for young Black lives in the inner city. I have written this book for them. One of them, Michael, wanted to know why it felt and seemed as though Black people were always at the bottom, and that young Black people from the block were often caught up and caught out but never catching a break.

I also wrote this book for Nico, my nineteen-year-old nephew who died in February 2016, several days after being stabbed. I need to record who he was, and for that record to be recognised beyond those of us who love him and miss him; for that record to be acknowledged by those who refuse to, or who seem unable to, understand that Black lives matter. Nico's life mattered. His story could have had a different outcome. When everything is taken away, including hope, these life-changing losses are destined to be endlessly repeated.

Neoliberalism ushered in free markets, deregulation of financial controls, and a move away from state intervention.

Forty years on, the notion of the state as a safety blanket in case of hard times has long been forgotten. Hyper-individualism is now the name of the game. In neoliberal times, the most brutal lie is meritocracy, the idea that everyone can "make it". That to "make it" you just have to keep at it and work hard. Meritocracy is a fabrication that masks inequalities and obstacles to success.[1] Our contemporary capitalist system is set up so that in order for some to make it to the top, the majority must remain at the bottom. Those at the bottom are then expected to take full responsibility for being in a position where the rules of the game are neither within their control, nor of their making. For many, the gap between those two positions has become an almost unbridgeable chasm.

On the horizon, however, is the hope that can come from creativity. Even in this harsh landscape, young people continue to make music that matters to them. Grime music emerged from east London in the early years of the twenty-first century, made possible by the resourceful activities of predominantly Black working-class communities. Making and listening to music is an integral part of young lives in Newham, so the social, economic and cultural significance of grime as a creative practice is woven into the fabric of this book.

This book, *Terraformed*, is my attempt to connect the dots, to locate our pains and our struggles, our wins and our losses in a structural, institutional and historical context. In this way, young people who have grown up under the influence of neoliberalism can articulate their stories as part of a community, not just as individual losses or gains. The Class of '91 are acutely aware, from the questions they raised, the passing comments, the discussions that we had, that "this England" is not working for them. Matt, Chris, Michael, and Amy are trying to understand not just "how it is" but "how it is *for them*". Young people are touched by increased levels of diagnosed anxiety and depression — how does this relate to the lived experiences of being poor in an affluent world, of feeling trapped and stuck? The sense of loss is palpable when your people (parents, siblings, friends), are removed from your life in some way or another; dead, deported, in custody, or incarcerated. These types of losses are so commonplace that when young Black Londoners make a reference to someone being "in", they don't mean at home, they mean in prison. Families are ruptured and friendships are constrained by rules of association, local policies and processes. Between them Matt, Chris, Michael, and Amy have had it all: huge student debt, invisible homelessness, custodial sentences, electronic tagging, surveillance, arrest, ASBOs, issues with health and well-being, and of course, loss. At a young age, they had witnessed and experienced extreme violence in the public arena. Some of this physical and verbal violence was at the hands of those who were supposed to protect them — i.e. the police. Symbolic violence came from teachers, and other authority figures who labelled, shamed and excluded them.

"Mask Off" is the title of a song by US rapper Future. He says "Fuck it", and then tells a story of trying to win when everything is pressing down on you. Future frames the lyrics within the context of using drugs to mask the harsh realities of everyday life. It's that sense of nihilism that I am addressing and providing a backdrop to. I could write about the exceptions, those that make it out unscathed somehow, but that tells us little about the everyday adversities that many young Black people go through. So, I am writing about what I see, without the mask of respectability, politeness and gratitude that has us almost beaten and reluctant to demand more.

Terraformed offers an insider ethnography of a square mile in a Newham neighbourhood — Forest Gate. It offers

3

an up close and personal perspective on how a newly arrived kinetic elite is able to move freely in this urban space. But there is another less visible landscape, where many young people have been rendered out of time and out of place. Operating almost on a parallel plane, less than half a mile from the weekly artisan market frequented by the new residents, a fourteen-year-old schoolboy receives a fatal gunshot wound to the head.[2] Five months earlier, a few streets away, a twenty-five-year-old man survives a drive-by shooting incident.[3]

According to sociologist C. Wright Mills, we cannot understand the life of an individual or the history of a society without understanding both.[4] These stories are located in a context of enduring inequalities, with rising housing costs, precarious employment, insecure housing, exclusion from the labour market, and rising levels of anxiety and depression, particularly among the young. For Black youth in these marginalised communities, matters of vulnerability are embodied and ever present.

The focus of this book is Forest Gate; an urban area in Newham, east London. Within that area, I concentrate on an approximate one-mile radius from Forest Gate station towards Wanstead Flats, and including part of the high street. All of the images included are photographs taken on my mobile phone as I walked around the area. During the planning and writing of this book, several shops closed down as the high street was undergoing redevelopment. A few shops moved further along, others closed down altogether. Some images are of particular incidents — for example after a nighttime police chase when gunshots were fired.

Terraformed is a series of essays. I have developed a new theoretical framework — *hyper-local demarcation* — as a way to analyse how the interaction between people, legislation, policy, the built environment and the sonic landscape offers a glimpse into the power relations that support inequalities and create exclusionary spaces.

I position this work within the context of Professor Christina Sharpe's concept of the wake.[5] What I mean by this is that I am keeping watch; observing and documenting how Black being continues as a form of consciousness, illustrating how Black youth survives and resists ongoing exclusion. Part ethnography, part memoir, this book contextualises the history of Newham and considers how young Black lives are affected by the impact of racism, neoliberal policies, and austerity.

CHAPTER ONE
NEWHAM: PAST AND PRESENT

Starting Out

Newham is an urban, multicultural London borough. It lies five or so miles to the east of the City of London's financial district. In contrast to the great wealth of the City, Newham has been a poor area for a long time. Formed out of the merger of East Ham and West Ham county boroughs in 1965, Newham illustrates the changing fortunes of the inner city in the last four decades. Now, it is striving to be a better place, aiming to improve housing and job opportunities, as well as aspiring to be an area where, according to its recent strapline, "people live, work and stay".

I have lived in Forest Gate on and off for many years, before mobile phones, digital television and social media. My first job, when I left school, was in Newham. In those days, most working-class children left school at sixteen and went to work. In the late 1970s, I turned up for work in a Civil Service department as a sixteen-year-old with no lived experience of the East End. I worked as a clerk in Stratford, processing paperwork for the goods imported into the UK. As an organisation, the Civil Service at that time was tightly structured with rigid hierarchies. Boundaries between roles and grades were clearly demarcated, with a sharp divide between manual workers, clerks, and the executive officers. There were very few Black staff and all but one had jobs in clerical or manual grades. Henry was an exception as he was an executive officer. A tall, forty-something, Black man, he had migrated from the Caribbean in the late 1950s. Henry's whole affect oozed gratitude for the job, the level, and the opportunity.

A daily routine was already in place when I arrived. Every morning, all of the white male staff would invoke a monkey chant, complete with Tarzan noises. It was a violent, unsubtle performance of overt racism. The younger men would start and then the rest would join in as the chorus. Every day as Henry walked in, they would do this — one to two minutes of gestures and chanting. Henry would always respond in the same way, he would smile at them benevolently, walk over to his desk, and unfold his newspaper — the *Financial Times*. After carefully noting down the currency exchange rates, Henry would start his day's work to the sound of ape noises. One day I asked him: "How do you stand it? Why do you put up with it?" I received this response from a self-identified "old colonial": "Remember, we are guests here my dear".

Grounded as I was in a reggae musical tradition of equal rights and justice, I had neither the desire for, nor interest in, being a guest. Some months later — as a not at all grateful sixteen-year-old, fed up with the constant racial and sexual harassment from an older white male colleague, I complained to the manager — seeking justice and a resolution. Within days, and without even speaking to the other party, I was transferred out to a different office in another part of Stratford. Nowadays, in our urban multicultural city, it is perhaps difficult to imagine such an obvious display of racist language and behaviours — although since Brexit, these incidents are on the rise.[1] Forty years ago though, Newham was a very different place, and incidents like these were commonplace.

Most of the paperwork and document filing that I did as part of my job in the Civil Service related to goods that came in via the Royal Docks, at that time one of the biggest employers in the area. As I stamped reference numbers and pinned (not stapled) different coloured pieces of paper to various forms, I gave no thought to the local and national significance of the docks in Newham, but thinking about the historical context of Newham as a location brings Britain's global imperialist and colonialist endeavours into sharp focus. Its diverse population reflects Britain's intrusive adventures in other lands. In the 1970s and 1980s, Newham had pockets of far-right politics that took anti-black violence to the streets. Newham is, and has always been, a poor area — it has high rates of unemployment, ill health and crime.[2] More recently, rising house prices in other areas, regeneration, and improved transport links has meant that Newham has become a desirable area to live in. Compared to the rest of London, homes in Newham are affordable, especially for those with relatively well-paid work. Contemporary Forest Gate, which sits at the edge of Wanstead Flats — a vast green space — has seen the arrival of a more well-resourced group of residents, who can afford to buy homes.

East London, Newham, Forest Gate

When Charles Booth carried out his study into the levels of poverty in London in the late nineteenth century, east London was viewed as a foreign land, situated in the shadow of the wealth of the City and populated by communities of poor people and migrants.[3] The East End has historically had a reputation for widespread dereliction,[4] it was seen as a symbol of the dark side of the nation — despite prosperity elsewhere, inner and outer east London remained poor.

In the Victorian era, as the more well-off workers[5] moved out to the new eastern suburbs of Ilford, Leytonstone and Forest Gate, new arrivals moved inwards — to places such as Canning Town, Aldgate and Whitechapel, which left a uniformly poor, residual community.[6] Furthermore, the 1944 Abercrombie Plan made it easier for skilled workers to move to new towns such as Harlow, leaving behind the "unskilled, semi-skilled, old and sick".[7]

Built in 1855, the Royal Docks are in the south of the Borough, and made up of Royal Victoria, Royal Albert, and King George V. These docks were created to meet the demands of the expanding British Empire, as the West India Docks were at capacity. Funded by income from slavery, the West India Docks opened in 1802. It sped up the time it took for a ship, arriving from the West Indies with goods such as rum, sugar and coffee — all made by slave labour — to unload and reload, thereby increasing profits.[8] Historian Hakim Adi describes London as a major port that sent slave ships, and slave produced goods, to Africa and the Americas — a traffic in human beings that brought great wealth to rich and powerful Europeans.[9]

By the 1880s the Royal Docks were operating as the largest docks in the world. Linked to a new and expanding railway network, they were able to take in the largest ships. Shipments of grain, tobacco, meat, fruit, and vegetables fuelled Britain's economic growth, importing from colonies such as India, Australia, and New Zealand. The Royal Docks ceased trading in 1981, and this was followed by a long period of economic decline.

Historically, because of its proximity to the docks, from the mid-nineteenth century Newham had a great deal of large-scale factory production. New, large factories were built in Silvertown for the bulk handling of sugar, grain, and rubber. Dozens of firms manufacturing metals, chemicals, textiles, furniture, food, drink, and tobacco were based in the area. These firms provided plenty of work, but it was noisy, malodorous and dangerous. The areas closest to the docks are Canning Town, Silvertown, and Plaistow. The population in these locations grew, as people moved in from around the UK and overseas to find work in the factories and at the docks. By the 1930s, Canning Town had the largest Black population in the country, and was home to the Coloured Men's Institute.[10]

As it was less suitable for heavy industry, Forest Gate, in the north of the Borough, housed clothing manufacturers and small workshops.[11] The street directory for 1903-1904 shows that Woodgrange Road and the main roads that run off it (Sebert Road, Forest Lane, and Dames Road) contained a variety of shops including: John Kettle; Grocers, TW Driver; Ham and Beef Warehouse, Walter Egbert; Florist, Ward and Co; Tailors (now a deli/pizzeria, estate agent, organic bulk store, cafe, and coffee shop respectively).

Forest Gate started out as a hamlet (a settlement smaller than a village) to the east of Stratford. Woodgrange Road, the main thoroughfare, takes its name from the site of Woodgrange Farm, a twelfth-century settlement. The roads to the east and west of Woodgrange Road had large houses, some triple-fronted and with servants' quarters. Some of the roads are named after Queen Victoria's palaces (Balmoral, Claremont, Windsor, Osborne and Hampton).

At the corner of Woodgrange Road and Forest Lane is Forest Gate Station, which opened in 1841, one of the first stations on the Eastern Counties Railway Line. The central point of market place at the junction of Forest Lane and Woodgrange Road was marked by the drinking fountain and clocktower. At the other end of Woodgrange Road, opposite Dames Road, is Wanstead Park Station, on the Barking to Gospel Oak Line. North of the railway in the streets off Forest Lane, the mainly terraced housing was built for clerks and skilled workers. An Industrial School on Forest Lane provided a fresh-air environment for inner-city children. In 1897 it became a workhouse, and then a hospital from 1929, until it was regenerated in 1986 to become a housing estate. Originally a Unitarian settlement, Durning Hall Community Centre is located at the junction of Woodgrange Road and Earlham Grove. It was rebuilt after being bombed in the Second World War. Durning Hall is the site for many community sports and leisure activities.

Migration Stories

As a multicultural area, it is evident that Newham has a long history of movement and migration; its population is made possible by Britain's colonial project. Although Britain used violence and terror to colonise large sections of the globe, popular discourse, on the whole, omits this aspect. At its height, the British Empire controlled almost a quarter of the world's population. The colonialist "scramble for Africa" was driven by a desire for new markets and raw materials. Conquest of the continent was made possible by technological advances (improved drugs that allowed Britons to survive tropical climates) and violence (machine guns that overpowered African weaponry). According to Historian David Olusoga, one in three Africans (forty-five million people) became British Colonial subjects.[12] Britain's heavy involvement in the slave trade meant that by the seventeenth century it also imported large numbers of Black people as chattel for sale to plantation owners in the Caribbean. Jamaica, for example, operated as a slave plantation for 150 years. Plantations were total institutions specialising in the production of sugar for export. A clear connection exists between Britain's colonial past and Newham's current population. Newham's residents with an Afrodiasporic heritage reflect Britain's global imperialist footprint. Academic Adam Elliot-Cooper puts it this way:

> Black Britain, possibly more than any African diasporic population on the planet, is incredibly diverse. It consists of people that hail from a range of Caribbean islands, from cultural powerhouses like Jamaica, to tiny protectorates, like Monserrat. Increasingly, Black people in Britain have migrated from the African continent, from former British colonies like Nigeria and Kenya, but also places like Congo or Somalia...[13]

Reports of imperialist adventures on the African continent and in the Caribbean reinforced the notion of black people as primitives in need of civilising. Scientific explanations for "race" positioned white Europeans as superior and by extension British people came to see themselves in the same way. Preconceptions of Africa and the Caribbean were shaped by colonialist ideas that associated black skin colour with savagery. World Fairs and Exhibitions contained human zoos, as well as exemplar "native villages". A handbill from 1895 for "Africa at the Crystal Palace" promises a "a native display of sixty-five picturesque natives of Somaliland".[14]

By the early twentieth century, Forest Gate had a large Jewish population that had moved out from the inner East End of London. For the most part, this population has moved on and no longer has a significant presence, but residual signs remain in the former Synagogue in Earlham Grove (on the map it is the first right turn after Forest Gate Station). By the end of the Second World War, there were twenty thousand Black people living in Britain in total —

mainly in the port areas of Liverpool, Glasgow, Cardiff as well as London's East End.[15]

After the Second World War the UK needed labour — almost a million workers were required to rebuild the country. An emerging welfare state, set up to provide a safety net for the British population in times of hardship, also needed workers. The 1949 British Nationality Act gave British subjects from the Commonwealth the right to enter and settle in the UK. Nationalised industries and private corporations actively sought out workers from the Caribbean, for example, London Transport, National Health Service, and the British Hotels and Restaurants Association, recruited in Jamaica and Barbados.

For Caribbean migrants, Newham may not have been their first choice, but it offered employment and cheap, albeit poor quality housing. Other UK areas had established Caribbean communities, with Jamaicans going to Notting Hill and Brixton, for example.[16] In the 1950s, Black and Asian mostly male migrants came looking for manual employment in the many factories in the Newham area. Employment was available around the Royal Docks, but not on the docks themselves due to racist, restrictive work practices that kept Black workers out.[17]

From the 1950s onwards, there was increased Caribbean migration to major cities in the UK. A colonial past meant that the British population had absorbed the centuries old constructions of "race". The British reaction to mass Black migration in the 1950s was not wholly favourable, and as Sheila Patterson wrote at the time, the "coloured migrants, particularly the Negro, appears to be the supreme and ultimate stranger".[18] Pretty soon, a cautious welcome gave way to overt anti-Black hostility.[19] Asian migration from east Africa reached a peak when, in August 1972, President Idi Amin ordered 55,000 Asians in Uganda to leave within three months. Several countries, including Britain, took in people who were now stateless.[20] In a debate in the House of Commons about what support could be given to the Ugandan Asians once they arrived, Arthur Lewis, the MP for West Ham North said:

> By all means let us help the Ugandan Asians in every possible way; let us prepare to help the Kenyan Asians when they come, as they will; but let us also help the people who are already here and have been suffering hardships for years.[21]

Black African migration to the UK started later than that from the Caribbean or South Asia. Small numbers arrived up to the 1990s, and then, at the turn of the twenty-first century, the number of migrants began to increase, particularly from West and Central Africa.[22] Asylum applications from sub-Saharan Africa increased due to war, civil unrest and conflict in Zimbabwe, Somalia, Eritrea, and Sudan.[23] According to the Migration Observatory, asylum applications increased from 1987 to 2002, and then reached a peak (of about 110,000) in the early 2000s. Most initial applications are refused. Strong measures to control applications have been put in place, and by 2018, the number of asylum applicants has dropped considerably to 44,200. 32% of these were nationals of Asian countries, 29% nationals of African countries, 26% nationals from Middle Eastern countries, and 10% from Europe.[24] Currently, Newham is responsible for less than six hundred asylum seekers.[25]

Today, Newham is one of the most multicultural boroughs in the UK. In Forest Gate North, which is the focus of this book, the resident population at the last census was made up as follows: 21% White British, 13%

Black African, 11% Bangladeshi, 8% Black Caribbean and 3% Mixed White and Black Caribbean/Black African.[26]

Housing

Newham experienced heavy bombing during the Second World War — between 7th October 1940 and 6th June 1941, 1,240 high explosive bombs were dropped on it.[27] A lasting impact of these bombing raids was not only that the physical landscape was destroyed, but working-class traditions and culture changed as residents moved away to the suburbs and south Essex. Major housing redevelopments and slum clearances from the late 1960s onwards, aimed at ridding the area of poorly-built dwellings, also resulted in population movements. Housing stock was dilapidated and often overcrowded, and high-rise blocks were built as a speedy solution to the borough's housing problems. In 1968, Ronan Point, a twenty-two-storey tower block in Canning Town, collapsed following a gas explosion, killing four people and injuring seventeen.

Housing was provided by the local council but it was in short supply, cheaply built and poorly maintained. A 1967 Housing Report stated that Newham had the biggest number of slums in the country.[28] Newham Council housing policy ensured that Black residents had little access to council housing by imposing a five-year residence requirement (in Greater London) as well as one year's residence in Newham, while the "Points System" prioritised those with long residencies. Newham Councillor Bill Watts said at the time: "It's justified because if changes are not made, in a few years' time we would have done nothing but give homes to Asians".[29] These types of housing policies made racism seem acceptable. Therefore, as council housing was not really an option for Black people in 1960s and 1970s, many turned to private accommodation, most of which was located in the north of the borough in areas such as Forest Gate.

In Forest Gate, small housing estates were built off the high street to replace the homes that had been destroyed by bombing. Although there had been improvements, housing on the whole was still of poor quality. By 1981, 30% of households still shared a bathroom, and 20% shared a toilet.[30] In terms of housing tenure, in 1981 30,000 homes were owner-occupied, 29,000 local authority homes, and around 14,000 private rented accommodation. By 2011, the Right to Buy legislation had taken its toll, and the number of local authority homes available had fallen to 18,000, whilst private rented accommodation had risen to 47000, and the number of owner-occupied homes had increased to 35,000.[31]

Economic Decline

Globalisation and technological advances, which meant that multinational companies could move parts of their operations overseas to lower wage economies,[32] meant that Newham, like many inner-city, areas lost its manufacturing base and experienced deindustrialisation. From the 1960s onwards there was an economic downturn and many jobs were lost. By the 1980s, the unemployment rate in Newham was at 20%.[33] Changes in global trading patterns meant that, in the south of the borough, the docks were no longer viable, and the Docklands area could not compete with the new container ports at Tilbury and Felixstowe. Sugar industry trade decreased as former British colonies gained their independence and developed their own sugar processing plants. In 1967 Tate and Lyle, a major employer in the borough, closed its processing plant in Plaistow; the plant in Canning Town remained but on a smaller scale. Old, outdated factories could not keep up with technological change and soon became redundant. With automation, fewer workers were needed. Jobwise, Newham was in steady decline. In 1981, the Royal Docks closed permanently, having become largely obsolete due to the bigger ships and the introduction of containers. Michael Heseltine, the Environment Secretary at the time, created the London Docklands Development Corporation (LDDC) to replace local authority control over the Docklands area — including the Royal Docks. The newly formed LDDC then bought up large areas of land for redevelopment.[34] When it finished in 1998, Docklands had an improved transport infrastructure — with the introduction of the Docklands Light Railway (DLR) — as well as an airport and a new financial district.

Across the borough, Newham continues to undergo a period of extensive regeneration and redevelopment, with plans to create 35,000 jobs, and 4,000 new homes in the Royal Docks alone.[35] In Stratford, the former Olympic Park has been redeveloped and may provide "40,000 jobs by 2025".[36] Forest Gate Station is also on the new Crossrail route — covering sixty miles, Crossrail, later to be known as the Elizabeth Line, will run from Reading via Heathrow in the west to Shenfield in the east.[37]

However, by any measure, Newham still faces economic and social challenges.[38] Residents are employed mainly in occupations that are relatively low-paid, including health, care and retail. Forest Gate reflects the profile of Newham as a whole in terms of types of employment and salaries.[39]

Contemporary Racism: Community Resistance

Newham has had a strong tradition of left-wing politics underpinned by a solid trade union foundation, often with a commitment to international worker solidarity. At the same time, however, in the decades after the Second World

War, racial stereotyping and support for racial violence was overtly embedded in everyday lives and working practices. The National Front — a far-right political party that advocated the use of violence — was able to prosper in the area, particularly in a time of economic decline. In 1968, east London dockers went on strike in support of Enoch Powell, who had been sacked from the government after his infamous "Rivers of Blood" speech. In 1973, the National Front formed a trade union association and campaigned for the forced repatriation of Black workers and supported striking Tate and Lyle workers. In the General Election in 1974, five thousand Newham residents voted for the National Front, giving them their largest vote in the country.[40] Newham, as we can see, was an area that contained both far-right as well as left-wing political enclaves.

According to sociologist Malcolm James, for many Black and Asian youth during this time, Newham was a highly problematic place where physical and verbal violence was an everyday occurrence.[41] In the south of the borough particularly, beatings and attacks on Newham's Black and Asian population continued, with schoolchildren particularly vulnerable to attack.[42] As Black children were viewed as a threat to social cohesion, a high rate of exclusions and perceived behavioural problems led to a disproportionate number of Black children being categorised as Educationally Sub Normal (ESN).[43]

During the 1970s and 1980s, racist street-level violence, sometimes instigated by far-right politics, appeared to be the norm. In 1977, Akhtar Ali Baig was killed in East Ham in a racially-motivated attack. Self-defence organisations, such as The Newham Defence League and Newham Monitoring Project, formed as a response to these continued attacks.[44]

Another way that racism and discrimination manifested itself was in the social sphere. Black people were routinely denied entry into public spaces — pubs and clubs were off limits, effectively a colour bar was in operation. Social divisions were clearly in evidence, with pubs as white spaces, and Black people socialising at house parties or community events. When those spaces came up against each other, violence often ensued. For example, in 1988, in an attack by white partygoers, Trevor Ferguson was left blinded in one eye after being hit with a bottle.[45]

After 1978, the election of Margaret Thatcher as Prime Minister ushered in a new era of politics. The extreme ideas of Enoch Powell and his ilk became absorbed into the government of the day. A "common sense" narrative around immigration was invoked, with natural Britons' reasonable fear of being "swamped" at the fore. But despite this hostile environment, Black communities established themselves — Newham began to flourish as a multicultural space where young people in particular co-existed in a somewhat edgy conviviality.

Twenty-First-Century Newham: Forest Gate

Newham is close to the UK's major financial districts — the City of London and Canary Wharf — but it is also a location where extreme wealth and naked poverty sit side by side. Owned by a global Canadian-led consortium, London City Airport, an international airport in the south of the borough, services growing numbers of wealthy business travellers. In a further effort to regenerate the area, Newham has been branded as a "Growth Borough". In Growth Boroughs, people tend to "die younger, earn less and are more likely to be unemployed".[46] In Newham, as in many urban marginal areas, young people are more vulnerable to the vagaries and fluctuations of the labour market: the occupational sectors where they are likely to find work are fragmented and insecure with high levels of casualisation, low pay and zero-hour contracts.[47]

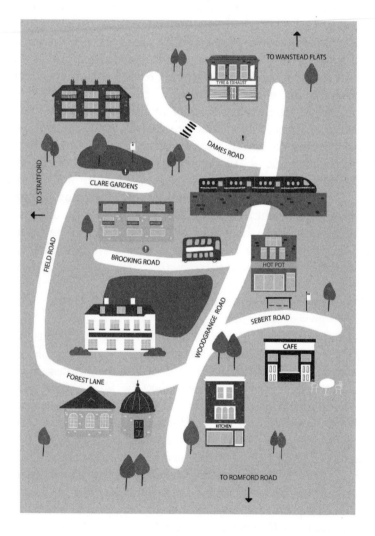

Figure 1: Stylised map of the square mile in Forest Gate — including the urban village

Although Newham has a long history of migration and movement, it has been constructed and imagined as a white area.[48] Nevertheless, despite an East End history that is rooted in a fictive white community that "extends from Bethnal Green in the east to Barking and Dagenham in the far east",[49] Newham is recognisably and notably multicultural. In Forest Gate it is possible to see the traces of past and present communities, and of past and present struggles. For example, the community organisation ELBWO (East London Black Women's Organisation) — set up in 1979 to provide childcare, advocacy, and legal advice for Black women — is now housed in the Methodist Church in Woodgrange Road.

At the junction where the main roads meet is where you will find many of the cultural and social spaces for the new Forest Gate residents — a weekly farmers market, coffee shops, and a gastropub offering a wide range of activities (see map). Another popular performance space is located under the railway arches, which is within Forest Gate but just outside the boundary for the London Borough of Newham. There are some outliers — a pizzeria/deli further down the high street, a craft beer spot under the railway arches off Sebert Road, and an organic bulk store where people can bring their own containers to buy produce such as grains, flour, fruit and vegetables (see map).

All of these leisure activities are in keeping with a local development framework within which the "regeneration of Forest Gate is a key priority for Newham Council".[50] For Forest Gate, this means the creation of a more genteel night-time economy, with a broader range of pubs, restaurants and cafes. Plans include Forest Gate becoming a site for small-scale business start-ups, as well as creative and cultural workspaces.[51] Newham also aims to deter crime and anti-social behaviour in the area by designing spaces and places that allow both "informal" and "natural" surveillance. An area off the main high street has been identified as a space that contains "backland areas and alleyways [...] that are considered to be hotspots for crime and environmental crime"[52] — the council aims to eradicate "backland" spaces like this.

Bigga,[53] who is of Caribbean heritage, grew up in Forest Gate in the 1970s. In 2019, we met in the pub that lies at the heart of the area. As he surveyed the interior and the surroundings, Bigga reflected on moving to Forest Gate (from Canning Town) in 1974. He said:

> It's not until you reflect on it that you realise how potent the racism was. We lived on a council estate, we were the only Black family in the block. Racism in those days was about the gaze, the way you were looked at, the way you were spoken to, the way you were made to feel. I remember the NF (National Front) signs were everywhere, swastikas, everywhere. It's really interesting to see how the area has changed.

I had been to this pub twice before — more on that in Chapter Four — but this was Bigga's first visit in its new guise. We found it to be calm, warm and welcoming, although not very ethnically mixed. When we sat in the courtyard at the back, we could see Bigga's former secondary school. By the late 1980s and early 1990s, Bigga had moved away from the area, and I no longer worked in Stratford. Together, we reminisced about Newham past, one with reggae sound systems, pool tournaments, and rowdy pubs with a strong sense of community.

Conclusion

In the past, Forest Gate was a wealthy suburb comprised of a well-to-do professional class. After the Second World War, in keeping with the rest of Newham, Forest Gate housed Black and Asian migrants. Later waves of migration came from Nigeria, Ghana, Somalia, Zimbabwe as a response to war, unrest and economic uncertainty. By the 1990s, Newham had become one of the most multicultural and diverse boroughs in the country, however, it is also a place of contrasts and contradictions. A solid, socialist history ran in parallel with far-right nationalist politics, which in the 1970s and 1980s sometimes spilled over into street violence.

British views on Black people were fired by imperialism and scientific racism — Black people were seen as the supreme and ultimate strangers. The Royal Docks, as well as being a source of English pride, locally and nationally, was built by slave labour in the Caribbean. Points of struggle and conflict occurred over housing as good quality housing was scarce, particularly after the bomb damage suffered in the Second World War. A decline in manufacturing meant that jobs were also at a premium, and Black workers were carved out of the meagre job opportunities that were available. Anti-Black and anti-Asian sentiment was strong and reflected in formal institutions and everyday encounters. Racial terror played out in the form of physical violence, chants, name calling, and sometimes death.

Nevertheless, in the 1970s, and the 1980s, communities came together and organised, in the workplace, in local politics, in schools and in housing services. They fought the worst excesses of racist Newham, and laid the foundations to challenge the spatial, verbal and physical expressions of inequality. Forest Gate today is a place of contrasts, highly desirable in terms of housing, transport connections and urban multicultural living, but at the same time a site of economic and social inequality.

CHAPTER TWO
NEOLIBERAL TIMES

In July 2016, while I was travelling on a train from Forest Gate to Stratford, I overheard a brief snatch of conversation. Two young Black men were discussing two recent events: the fallout from a water fight in Hyde Park which resulted in a number of altercations and several arrests,[1] and a Black Lives Matter march through central London that had taken place earlier in the month.[2] As they were leaving one of them said:

> Black lives don't matter, we are the ones that are killing each other [...] it's Black people killing Black people, so I don't give a fuck...

How did we get here, where urban life compels some young people to exist on a nihilistic plane, where no one cares and nothing matters? In marginalised communities, like the London Borough of Newham where the above exchange took place, systemic and symbolic violence flows through from the school to the street as standard practice. We bear witness to it daily. Ghetts is a highly acclaimed grime MC and independent recording artist from Plaistow in Newham. In an interview with *Channel 4 News* in September 2018, he responded to a question about the supposed, and often repeated, link between knife crime and grime music. He said:

> I'm a mirror, I'm reflecting what's going on. Stay in this neighbourhood for 24 hours, then draw what you see.

He talks about loss and being a witness to violence, and implores those of us that are from here, that have a level of understanding, to explain what is really happening to young people in poor areas.

Lived experiences, musical creative expression, policy and literature, allow us to explore the experiences of young lives with a Black diasporan or Afrodiasporan cultural heritage and enables us to go beyond what the quantitative data tells us about housing, employment and violent crime. If we look at a tightly defined geographical area, like Forest Gate, it is possible to recognise how social and economic inequalities are produced and reproduced. Local policy strategies for Forest Gate to allow us to identify planned methods for economic growth, redevelopment[3] and regeneration.[4]

Forest Gate as it stands today is a complex mesh of gentrification, inequality, everyday multiculturalism, and violence which is simultaneously symbolic, structural and slow. These strands, underpinned by a neoliberal agenda, form the fabric of Forest Gate residents' parallel lives.

Neoliberal Times

Until the early 1980s, the welfare state in the UK operated as an interventionist endeavour. It redistributed wealth, managed unemployment levels, and tried to counter social inequality. After the Second World War, a political consensus emerged that promoted a mixed economy in which, together, the private sector and the government provided goods and services. The government took over the running of many key services (such as water, energy, and the railways), and cut the link between a person's social needs and their ability to pay for those needs — on the whole this meant that health, social care and education, for example, were free at the point of service. This interventionist approach meant that the state curtailed the private sector's worst excesses, giving citizens and workers much needed protection.

A series of economic crises in the mid-1970s ushered in the end of this post-war consensus and saw the emergence of neoliberalism. Based on the premise of individual freedom unfettered by government and a much reduced welfare state, the neoliberal project goes back some forty years. Over time, its ideology, that a "free market economy" — where the private sector is primarily responsible for providing goods and services — was the best way for social and economic progress, gradually became common sense.[5] As leader of the Conservative Party, Margaret Thatcher was elected Prime Minister in 1979, and ushered in a series of free market policies influenced by economists like Friedrich Hayek and Milton Friedman, as well her desire for a strong state in terms of law and order.

Under her leadership, and those of the neoliberal governments that followed, we saw the UK transform into a society that prized individual endeavour for individual reward, rather than communal effort for societal gain. Her "right to buy" legislation allowed tenants to buy their council homes at a significant discount, enabling large sections of the UK population to became part of a "property owning democracy", reducing the council housing stock. Nationalised industries were sold off, as an ideological move, and as a way to give the general population the opportunity to become share owners as well as home owners. Post-Thatcher, successive Conservative governments extolled the virtues of competition and continued to privatise previously nationalised industries. Tony Blair's New Labour maintained the ideology that the free market was the best way to provide cost-effective public services. Privatisation occurred either through the direct sale of a public service, or by outsourcing — bringing the private sector into the delivery of public services. In this way private sector principles of cost efficiency and competition entered into the public sector. As a process, outsourcing continued under New Labour, the Coalition government from 2010, and the subsequent Conservative government.

The sheer scale of public sector services that have moved into private hands is immense. Thinking about the reach of the private sector over the last forty years, there are few areas that remain untouched. For example, in the 1980s the government sold off British Aerospace, British Telecom, car manufacturers Jaguar and Rolls Royce, British Rail, British Gas, and British Steel. More recently, aspects of the Probation Service, the Prison Service, the NHS, and schools are being provided by private companies.

In November 2018, forty years on from the advent of neoliberal policies, Philip Alston, the UN Special Rapporteur on Extreme Poverty and Human Rights, toured the UK. Over a two-week period, he visited different locations, taking written submissions on the challenges that people faced. One of these locations was the London Borough of Newham. Alston found that in the UK in 2019, despite being the fifth richest economy in the world, "food banks have proliferated; homelessness and rough sleeping have increased greatly; tens of thousands of poor families must live in accommodation far from their schools, jobs and community networks; life expectancy is falling for certain groups and the legal aid system has been decimated".[6]

In Forest Gate, on Woodgrange Road and just outside the square mile that is the focus of this book, there is a former BT office block. Now owned by an offshore company, it has been developed into temporary accommodation for Newham's homeless families. It's a lucrative business for the firm, which charges a nightly rate, but tenants — including children — live with mould, mice, and damp.[7]

In nearby Stratford, Europe's biggest shopping centre and luxury student accommodation, and a permanent tent city for rough sleepers exist within a few hundred metres of each other.

Crisis Talks

The 2008 global financial crisis had its origin in the US housing market, although it was also a symptom of a much deeper problem within the global financial system. An overreliance on complex, computer-based credit risk assessment meant that banks in the UK and the US were lending money to people who could ill afford to pay it back.[8] In the UK, the coalition government elected in 2010 used the crisis as an excuse to usher in a programme of austerity, sold initially as a temporary measure to bring about economic stability. As part of this programme, in a bid to cut costs, government policy committed to outsourcing more public services to private companies, as well making stringent spending cuts in the public sector, including to youth services. Youth unemployment rose, and at its peak there were almost one million unemployed 18-24 year-olds in the UK.[9] Some ethnic minority communities were hit particularly hard by the increase in youth unemployment — in 2013, 45% of Black youth were unemployed, compared with 18% of the white population.[10] Policy changes to welfare benefits, housing, and public services were wide-ranging; housing benefit was removed from young people under twenty-one, the benefit cap limited the amount of income that a household could receive, and university tuition fees tripled to £9,000 per year. These actions added to an already bleak picture for young people in the UK, particularly those from poor communities.[11]

So now, after almost a decade of austerity, underpinned by neoliberal policies, we are at a time of crisis. We are witnessing the breakdown of political apparatus, of capital, and of finance. Predatory capitalism has destroyed our capacity to care for each other in any meaningful way. Increasing numbers of people have precarious working lives, existing on zero-hour contracts and on or below the minimum wage. For the first time in decades, life expectancy in the UK has stalled, as research showed an increase in the number of deaths in 2015.[12] The Brexit debacle has masked the crisis brought about by austerity — for example, the number of rough sleepers has risen by 169%, and there is an increase in relative child poverty. Also, since 2010, a thousand Sure Start centres have closed, removing much needed support for low income families. Across the UK there has also been a significant rise in the use of food banks not just for those on benefits, but also for those in work.[13] It appears that despite saving money by cutting and outsourcing services, some councils — such as Northamptonshire County Council, Birmingham City Council and Barnet Council — are teetering on the edge of bankruptcy.[14]

Policies that crush the poor have been introduced with seemingly little resistance — the introduction of Universal Credit has left many benefit claimants in abject poverty, while Education Maintenance Allowance (EMA) and now maintenance grants have been taken away from the poorest students. In a recent paper that asks the question "Why is austerity governable?", Jonathon Davies et al analyse how, following the 2008 global financial crisis, local councils, ostensibly opposed to austerity, delivered savage and punitive cuts to services. Community resources have been depleted, hence the seeming lack of fight from those who are most affected by the austerity agenda. Social housing communities have been dispersed by the right to buy policy, an initiative that also stopped local authorities from building more homes. Subsequent housing policies have created short tenancies and transient communities.[15] A neoliberal approach is seen as common sense and disadvantage or poverty is understood at an individual level rather than at a structural one. In this landscape, big business enjoys light-touch regulation, while at the same time the general public is subject to increasing monitoring and surveillance.[16] Whatever the political stance of the government in power, over the last four decades, social problems have been dealt with through legislation.[17] The key point here is that once neoliberalism embeds private-sector culture and values into state institutions, the pursuit of profit becomes the driving force behind many public services. We have endured almost a decade of austerity, mainly directed at those with the least power and the most to lose — welfare benefits claimants, immigrants, and the poor. For many, life is a constant battle of rising living costs and stagnating income.

There is a crisis in deregulation; public services such as social work, health care, prisons, probation, and education have been outsourced, often to amorphous organisations that appear to have little accountability. These multinational businesses have caused repeated failures with the delivery of public services, but these companies, for the most part, continue to be handed huge contracts.

It's important to place these issues of outsourcing and privatization into a local context. Let's look at three private sector companies that provide public services in the London Borough of Newham — Carillion, Serco and G4S.

Carillion, Serco and G4S

Starting out as a construction company, Carillion demerged from the Tarmac group in 1991. It held a number of public service contracts, including supplying maintenance services to Network Rail and to homes for the Ministry of Defence, as well as managing schools, highways and prisons.[18] Carillion went into liquidation in January 2018 and many of its services have since been brought back into government control. In Newham, Carillion provided "soft" facilities management (catering, cleaning, and portering) at Newham University Hospital.

Barts Health NHS Trust provides clinical services to east London. It operates from four major hospital sites, including Newham University Hospital, and in a number of community locations. As the largest NHS Trust in England, it serves 2.5 million people and is a major employer in the area, employing 16,000 staff.

In 2018, Serco took over the former Carillion contracts at Barts Health. Serco provides health care services for six NHS Trusts including Barts Health, which covers Newham University Hospital and North East London Foundation Trust (NELFT), employing over 8,000 staff in cleaning, facilities management and clinical support. Hospitals have been absorbed into the world of finance and big business, seen as profit-making opportunities that form part of company business portfolios.

Serco, an outsourcing company founded and based in the UK, had revenues of £3 billion in 2017. An international operation, in Britain it manages six adult prisons, as well providing services to the NHS.[19] Since 2007, it has run Yarl's Wood, an immigration detention centre for foreign nationals facing deportation. It includes adult women and adult family groups who are required to have identity checks. In February 2018, more than 100 women at Yarl's Wood went on hunger strike in protest at the lack of adequate healthcare. The women also protested against the lengthy and disorganised processes which mean indefinite detention for many.[20] According to its website, Serco is "trusted to deliver critical support services and operate sensitive military facilities".[21]

In a speech to the Business Services Association in June 2018, Rupert Soames, Serco Group Chief Executive, gave a spirited defence of the practice of outsourcing. He said:

We who take the taxpayers' shilling operate only with political permission; it is not we who created our market. Our industry was created by an act of political will, supported by four pillars. The first pillar was a belief in a small, rather than large state, inspired by economic philosophers such as Hayek and Friedman. The second pillar was a practical observation that privately owned utilities such as AT&T and Hong Kong Telecom provided a better service than the then Post Office. The third was the pressing need to attract private capital for infrastructure investment which the state needed but could not finance. The fourth pillar was the arrogance of the public-sector unions who felt that they could create misery without consequence, and ineffective management of nationalised businesses such as British Rail who delivered lousy service...

He goes on to argue that handing the delivery of public services over to the private sector has revolutionised them, and that the policy, "enthusiastically" supported by thirteen years of New Labour governments, enabled "the creation of great wealth for the owners and managers of the privatised utilities, delivered billions of pounds of investment in our infrastructure, and spawned companies such as Capita and Serco which rose from nowhere to being in the FTSE-100..."

He railed against breaking the consensus that the private sector is best placed to deliver public services. Soames argued that calls for renationalisation, or "taking back the NHS", put companies such as Serco in "danger of losing the political permission to take the taxpayer's shilling and serve the public".[22]

Taking the taxpayers shilling and serving the public is well rewarded if you are at the top of the Serco tree. Rupert Soames received a £4.5million overall pay package in 2018.[23] By way of contrast, a prison custody officer in London earns a yearly salary of £26,000 for a forty-hour week, whilst a catering team leader earns £23,000.[24]

G4S is another significant provider of outsourced public services, and is also the world's largest private sector employer. In 2011 it was the first private contractor to run a jail — HMP Birmingham. However, after a number of crises, including a riot that lasted twelve hours, hundreds of assaults, rat infestations and widespread use of the drug spice,[25] control was returned to the Ministry of Justice in August 2018.[26] At the Secure Training Centres under their control there have been reports of inappropriate treatment of young people.[27] For example, at the Medway Secure Training Centre (children aged twelve to seventeen), there were not only allegations of physical and verbal abuse, but also claims that incidents were underreported so as not to incur a financial penalty.[28]

When, in 2012, G4S was given responsibility for the security at the London Olympics, chaos ensued on the Newham site, and G4S had to be replaced by the armed forces. Up to two weeks before the start of the Games there were "no schedules, uniforms or training on x-ray machines".[29] In 2017, G4S was investigated over claims of fraud in its electronic tagging contract — essentially, G4S had erroneously claimed payment for monitoring people who were dead or non-existent. G4S paid the money back, covering the cost of their error by issuing a £23.3 million credit note to the Ministry of Justice.[30] However, even a mistake of this magnitude does not impact on its ability to secure public money. As its remit is so wide, G4S has been deemed "too big to fail".[31]

Gentrification or Regeneration?

According to urban geographer Tom Slater, gentrification has become regeneration, occurring in areas that have previously been sites of disinvestment, places where the well-off moved out of, and businesses relocated from.[32] As a process, regeneration is more than residential rehabilitation — often people are displaced while the new developments are in progress, and sometimes they do not return. Socially, culturally and economically, existing residents have to make room for the newcomers. In Forest Gate, that displacement takes place in social and residential spaces. As previously undesirable environments become more sought after, power is conveyed in the use of social space, as what David Sibley calls "opaque instances of exclusion" are enacted in daily life, in the coffee shop, the deli, or the market.[33]

Newham Council's Supplementary Planning Document outlines its improvement plans for Forest Gate. The council wants to maintain the conservation area, improve the shopping facilities, tackle anti-social behaviour and improve the housing offer, while protecting the qualities that give Forest Gate its special flavour.[34] It aims to create the feel of a relaxed "urban village". The high street lies at the heart of this reinvestment and regeneration project. Newham has traditionally been framed as a multicultural area, and this is reflected in the shops in the high street. But its reframing as an urban village means that what now has cultural value is the coffee shop, the delicatessen and the artisan bakery.

Symbolic, Structural and Slow Violence

Since the 1980s, the UK has experienced widening inequality — poverty has become entrenched and the gap between rich and poor has become a gulf. Meanwhile, the ideology of neoliberalism means that individuals author their own success (or failure).[35] Politeness, respectability, gratitude and fear deter us from speaking out about what we see and what our lived experience tells us that we know. Austerity has hushed the voices of the poor, the disadvantaged and the marginalised. As civic participation often declines in more unequal societies,[36] it allows toxic policies to be implemented unchallenged. Some still speak up and speak out, the Focus E15 Campaign is one example,[37] but those that do protest may become subject to monitoring, surveillance, and punishment.[38]

In *Concerning Violence*, Frantz Fanon framed the city as a world cut in two, a world "divided into compartments" with different species occupying those compartments.[39] This framing serves as a useful starting point. In the newly gentrified areas of Forest Gate, the borders, enclaves and colonies are evident, but it is not a simple bifurcation. Fanon outlines the well-off colony or "settlers town" as a brightly lit place where people are well fed and protected from the elements. The well fed areas of Forest Gate in Newham have access to a wide range of resources, and a sense of community is drawn from shared activities and leisure sites. On the other hand, the backland areas and alleyways off the high street that are mentioned in the Planning Document are deemed less desirable, less spacious, and contain, according to the council, poor quality housing. There are increased levels of surveillance for these areas via neighbourhood policing and community support officers. The council uses street furniture and other disciplinary techniques to keep unruly, non-docile bodies from the areas of ill-repute in their place. When combined with the use of the ASBOs and the PSPOs, the agents and tools of government speak the language of force — bringing violence into the home and the mind.[40]

In *Slow Violence and the Environmentalism of the Poor*, Rob Nixon talks about "slow violence", a gradual, mainly invisible, destruction that is not spectacular or explosive but which happens across time and through space.[41] For David Graeber, "structures of violence" are the underpinning processes and techniques that make racism and poverty possible.[42] Austerity measures have forced (and encouraged) local councils to crush and reshape the public sector and social services; outsourcing staff and contracting out services. It is within this context that levels of serious youth violence appear to be escalating. We can see this in the number of young people who are dying as a result of a knife attacks — 2018 was the worst in a year in England, in which 37 children and teenagers were stabbed to death.[43] My point is that the young Afrodiasporic population who are at the heart of this book experience symbolic violence, slow violence and structures of violence as an everyday experience, as a standard component of their daily lives that as they are under surveillance and rendered out of place.

Hyper-Local Demarcation

With this book I am trying to make sense of and contextualise matters of vulnerability and inequality in young Black lives. There are many sociological and political concepts we can use to understand and investigate the relationship between neoliberalism and austerity and their effects on people. For example, Sociologist Loic Wacquant's concept of "advanced marginality" is a useful tool to analyse the effect of the end of the post-war consensus and the introduction of neoliberal ideas.[44] Additionally, Michel Foucault's theories help us to understand the disciplinary techniques of power (including the control of the body at an individual level) and procedures of knowledge that are used to create different kinds of community and architectural space,[45] as well as allowing us to examine how some people become subject to state power in a way that they cannot counter and cannot identify. We could also consider what Foucault and Miskowiec call the *set* of relations, such as streets and transportation, which define a given site — for example, paying close attention to the *cluster* of relations such as cafes and cinemas that allow a site to be defined as a space of relaxation.[46] However, the nexus of poverty, racial division and post-colonial migration in the London Borough of Newham requires a more nuanced and specific reading. As we are talking about young Black lives, we also need to consider Christina Sharpe's concept of "the wake" and what it means to live with ongoing subjection and resistance as a historical and contemporary terror filtered, in the UK, through racism and a visibly hostile environment.[47]

To contemplate how power and resources are distributed, and to examine how racialised narratives of economics function locally, I want to put forward a framework — *hyper-local demarcation*. Using this framework allows us to examine how legislation, communities, the sonic landscape, and town planning come together at the level of the street and make an impact on young Black lives.

Legislation

In its broadest sense, the law operates as a system of rules, regulations that are designed, (with our permission) to control our behaviour. The legislative framework applies to all, however its application may mask racialised, systemic and structural violence. To maintain order and to control and monitor not just individuals but groups of individuals, environmental law, civil law, housing, mental health and immigration law are used. These laws turn on a "balance of probability" so the burden of proof is lower than in criminal proceedings. Implementing legislative practices in particular ways can limit access to services, curtail free choice, and detain those who have not broken any law.

Communities

A number of diverse communities occupy these streets in different ways. Leisure pursuits and use of public space are temporal and informed by housing tenure, as well as income. Community activities operate in parallel spaces informed by variables such as age, gender and ethnicity. When you look at who is attending the weekly ballet class, and who is chilling on the block, sharp divisions appear. Distinctions are also apparent in personal belongings and community activity.

Sonic Landscape

The musical backdrop is a distinct strand in the leisure pursuits and activities of particular communities. Music is used as a method to create sense of belonging, therefore, consideration should be given to the places where music is made and consumed. Consideration needs to be given also to whether there are connections between listening communities.

Town Planning

Local development plans have an impact on how space (public and private) is shaped and used. Residential and commercial interests have to be managed and aligned. The vision for the high street or the main thoroughfare provides a context for how space is divided and used.

Taken together, legislation, communities, the sonic landscape, and town planning allow us to really think about how young Black lives are experienced from the bottom up.

CHAPTER THREE
WHY MUSIC MATTERS

A fresh start thinking I should stay low
but it's when I moved to Forest Gate called a new place home
Started rapping thinking that I could be the next J.Cole[1]
But we were on the block posted up on Woodgrange Road
Like why do you think they call this place the Gaza[2]
You're not living how I'm living so how can you have the answers
— Baseman, "Better Place: Forest Gate"[3]

For some Newham residents, poverty is a part of everyday life. Having no money is hard work, and you pay more for everything — energy, phones, furniture and food all cost more when you cannot pay upfront or by direct debit. If you are on a low income, there is little capacity to deal with unexpected events. Many young people in Newham grow up in families where financial insecurity is the order of the day. Even though the east London area as a whole has changed, with rising house prices as well as the arrival of wealthier homeowners, entrenched hardship remains a reality for many. In measures of relative deprivation, Newham is ranked 8th, and although there have been some improvements, the overall picture is the same.[4] Young people in this area have had more than three decades of economic and social inequality.[5] After the global financial crisis in 2008, the UK government responded with a tough austerity programme, worsening the predicament of those from disadvantaged communities. In this neoliberal landscape individuals are expected to be solely responsible for their fate, even in the face of structural issues they come up against, such as unemployment, inequality or homelessness.

In many ways it is both inevitable and incredible that a musical genre like grime would come out of a place like Newham — a historically poor, predominantly young, performatively white but actually multicultural borough. The ongoing struggle is for those young people who want to do well, but encounter obstacles that lock them out of good quality work, or jobs with opportunities.

Introducing Grime and Rap as Musical Practice

At the start of the twenty-first century, Newham was a prime location for the emerging grime scene. Estates, street corners, youth clubs and schools operated as creative clusters where young people would gather to create their own innovative take on UK garage. At a time when artists such as Skepta (who won the Mercury Prize in 2016 with *Konnichiwa*) and Stormzy (an independent recording artist whose album *Gang Signs and Prayer* got to number 1 in 2017) are internationally known, it is easy to overlook the early work of Newham luminaries such as Sharky Major or Ghetts.[6] Produced through the convivial endeavours of young people of Caribbean, African and English heritage, and using a distinctive flow and regional accents, grime MCs rap or "spit" over a sparse 140-beats per minute (bpm) instrumental. Grime beats are in many ways a sonic representation of the spaces their creators occupy. Grime's sonic origins flow through the musical practice of the Black diaspora, namely hip-hop, reggae (particularly dancehall), jungle and, UK garage, whilst Jamaican and UK sound system culture and practice also had a significant influence. Inner-city teenagers, making music from the limited resources that they had around them, were the foundation of grime's early days. These young people drew on their cultural heritage from the Caribbean or Africa to create a hyper-localised sound that spread throughout the world.[7] Rap is also a Black vernacular cultural form, but with a slightly slower beat. Globally, rap is one of the most popular musical genres, and in the UK it has a longer history than grime, going back some thirty years.

With both of these musical genres it is possible to sustain a musical career without the input of an intermediary, such as a record company. For Black youth in particular, the contemporary music scene is a site of emancipatory disruption where it is possible to take on a new identity as an artist, a performer or an entrepreneur. In a socio-economic landscape that is beset by racism and inequality, this emancipatory aspect cannot be ignored.

Grime and rap form a musical backdrop to young life in east London. In the mid-2000s, both of these musical forms could be heard on public transport, in the street, and as ringtones on early mobile phones. Groups of young people moving around together, engaged in the banter that formed part of their musical practice, was a common sight. A decade ago, online, on YouTube and MySpace, it was possible to watch music videos, often recorded on mobile phones, where you could see young people putting in their practice hours, honing and perfecting their craft. Channel U (which later became Channel AKA) was a digital TV channel that became another affordable outlet to broadcast music videos, as long as you did not use profanities, and met the required standard in terms of quality. To get a video on Channel U, you needed to raise your game in terms of technical ability and skills, as the editing and sound quality needed to be of a high standard. Many of the music videos at that time had a very local feel, incorporating street signs and local landmarks such as train stations, parks, youth clubs, housing estates and fast food outlets.

A Sense of Belonging

One way that young people in Newham create a sense of belonging is through music. The contemporary genre of grime illustrates this point well. As a music genre that draws on a Black Atlantic cultural aesthetic,[8] grime has a sonic genealogy that has its origins in the east London boroughs of Newham and Tower Hamlets.[9] How and where the music is made reflects the divergent spatialities of inner-city environments.[10] Due to advances in technology, the availability of the Internet and the subsequent explosion of social media, grime has become a highly accessible musical genre. A music video can be created, uploaded and shared to an audience far beyond the local area. An added benefit is that young people with very few resources can interpose into any number of performing identities related to music, for example as MCs, DJs, producers, videographers, or event promoters.

In the UK, grime and rap exhibit a categorical engagement with place identities. Artists' lyrics referenced the areas that they came from and identified with. An initially hyper-local creative expression, by the mid-2000s grime was being disseminated to a much wider audience in the UK, Europe and North America.[11] Videos, made to promote and support a track, often featured local neighbourhoods and landmarks. In 2016, SBTV — the online youth broadcaster — developed a musical series called *Better Place*. It offered a platform to artists to talk about their hopes and dreams, as well as the challenges of coming from a particular area.[12] Two of these tracks relate to areas in Newham: Lil Nasty on Plaistow[13] and Baseman x Snizzy on Forest Gate.[14] In both, we are offered an uncompromising narrative about what it means to grow up poor with limited choices. Loss features strongly, but so does love.

We can see the role that grime, and other popular contemporary genres such as rap and UK drill, perform in the production of local identities, often working as art, literature and ethnography. These expressive, everyday practices offer modes of self-actualisation, or ways for young people to be all that they can be, as well as a means to critically reflect on feelings and emotions. In Newham, young people work individually and collectively to get their musical products out into the public arena — resources are shared, and friends and other members of the community might, for example, take part in the making and filming of a video. A strong link exists between music, place and identity; as Ray Hudson argues, "music has the ability to conjure up powerful images of place, and feelings of deep attachment to place".[15] Listening to the lyrics and absorbing the visuals in the Baseman x Snizzy's *Better Place* video shows that powerful and deep attachment to place. From the opening shots, we see local reference points in the public realm (see map) such as the park behind the former hospital in Forest Lane, as well as the high street, Forest Gate Station and the Caribbean takeaway. Young men come together in the video, some with their faces covered, as they gather in groups of various sizes, converging in twos or threes. As they walk alongside each other, talk and smoke together, kinship, brotherhood, and care is expressed, and at work. In this video lyrically and visually, Baseman x Snizzy provide a sense of place, locating us firmly in the area of Forest Gate.

Music Matters in Forest Gate

In Forest Gate North, Woodgrange Road is the spine that runs through the proposed urban village. In past times, this small area housed a number of entertainment venues; people's palaces and cinemas. The Forest Gate Public Hall, also known The People's Picture Palace, was set back slightly off the main road, situated between what is now a bakery and a pharmacy. It opened in 1902 but then it closed for good at the beginning of the Second World War. Later on, it had a new lease of life as a roller-skating rink, a clothing factory and then as The Upper Cut club. At its peak in the 1960s, it featured successful US artists including Jimi Hendrix and Stevie Wonder.[16] By the time I went there as a young adult in the mid-1980s, rollerskating had made a comeback, and there was the occasional local live reggae band, but there were few signs of its glorious past as a cinema and music venue. After a short period as an electrical store, it was demolished in 2005 to make way for a ventilation shaft for the Channel Tunnel rail link.

The roads off Woodgrange Road contain much sought-after Victorian housing. Double-fronted houses, some with former servants' quarters, line the streets that are named after Queen Victoria's palaces and castles: Hampton, Osborne, Claremont, Windsor, and Balmoral. Bomb damage during the Second World War meant that some of the houses were replaced with a small housing estate, four small blocks on Claremont Road, a low-rise estate called Davidson Terraces, and a eleven-storey tower block in Windsor Road. This little haven contained streets and spots that were popular with young people. My Class of '91 described this area with fondness, and talked about a particular spot that "we used to call the warm block", it was more comfortable to hang out there because it was less exposed to the weather. You could get to "warm block" by walking through the alley that runs between the supermarket and the pound shop. These were places where young people indulged in common youthful endeavours; meeting up, hanging out, and passing the time. By the mid-2000s, easier access to camera phones, camcorders and YouTube meant that making a music video for broadcast online was a popular and relatively cheap activity. At the same time as groups of predominantly Black youth were coming together in public to make music, policymakers and legislators began to make more of the imagined connection between youth (a dangerous time) and the streets (dangerous places),[17] with devastating consequences.[18]

Three locally made music videos — "Its ms – Promotional Hood Video" by Minisparks, "Who's That Click" by Woodgrange E7, and "Talks" by Baseman and Snizzy — created over an eight-year period, were filmed in the heart of the Forest Gate area that is the focus of this book. It is worth looking at these in more detail.

Minisparks — "Its ms – Promotional Hood Video" (2008)[19]

This video was filmed by a low-budget company to be uploaded to YouTube. It begins with silence for thirty-eight seconds as the shot pans across the police helicopter flying overhead. Roughly fifteen young men populate the video, which is set in the small housing estate behind the shops, one of these so-called "backland areas" described in the Forest Gate Development Plan.[20] There is one main MC, and the remaining group add substance by adlibbing and making the necessary gestures. At 1:08 there is an iconic shot: to the right are the garages, and the group of young men stand in front of a wall, in various poses. Two of them have bicycles. They wear the standard attire for the time — snapbacks, hoodies and baggy denim jeans. A solitary young man sits on the wall just behind the main group. Lyrically, the song is limited, but there are several references to E7 (the postcode for Forest Gate) and shots next to the Claremont Road street sign. The final frame shows a police car in Woodgrange Road itself, in front of the Methodist church. The video comes to an abrupt end at 3:06. It is a playful, unpolished effort, designed to show off the developing MC skills of the main character. In ten years, Promotional Hood Video has amassed almost eight thousand views and a single comment: "ard" (hard).

WoodGrange E7 — "Who's That Click" (2012)[21]

The "Who's That Click" video involves a large group of young Black men calling themselves "Who's That Click" — after the street at the centre of what is now the urban village. Forgoing a traditional grime beat, the MCs in this group rap their lyrics over the soundtrack of a 1990s American RnB song, reworking "Who's That Girl?" by Eve into "Who's That Click". As a host borough for the London 2012 Olympics, Newham was keen to protect its reputation, so this video was one of seventy-six removed by the council as part of a public safety initiative. In a counter move, the video was reposted in April 2013 with a disclaimer at the start stating that the views were the artists' own.

In the video, MC performance is interspersed with shots of people riding bicycles, a game of football, passers-by going about their daily business and patrolling police officers. It can be seen as a performance of youth culture that draws on both global and local references.[22] There are four main performers, with the remainder of the group providing the necessary adlibs, all adopting the normative style of swagger, gesture and pose. Common themes emerge — in the lyrics we hear about the primacy of the crew and about how hard life is in the neighbourhood. Visually, we see bicycles, clothing — hoodies, snapbacks — and a shot of the police and a police car. Some of the video is filmed on a basketball court a few streets away on a post-war council housing development. In the five-minute video, the four MCs consecutively weave a story of "real life" in Forest Gate. Like Baseman in the "Better Place" video, WoodGrange E7 make reference to Forest Gate being like Gaza.

Baseman x Snizzy — "Talks" (2016)[23]

"Talks" is a much more polished affair, and begins by referencing the news item relating to the removal of the "Who's That Click" video in 2012. Filmed and directed by videographer MayowaHD, the beat is softer, with tender female vocals, but it belies the harshness of the lyrics. A sense of play that is evident in the previous videos is absent and both protagonists seem weary. One MC wears a gas mask, possibly as an aesthetic gesture or perhaps as a disguise. The talk now is of trusting no one, and of Forest Gate being like a war zone. As the drone shot pans across, you can see the landmarks in Woodgrange Road, Forest Gate Station, the library and the supermarkets. One of the performers says, "Fuck the hood, I just wanna live lavish". Filmed from the rooftop of a former factory in Woodgrange Road (now luxury apartments) there are some scenes on the same basketball court that was used in the "Who's That Click" video. No police presence is apparent in this video.

The Significance of Music

In all three videos, the geographical location is visually and lyrically identifiable and referenced, sometimes by name as "Forest Gate", by its postcode as "E7", or by its local name "Woody" (for Woodgrange Road). All the tracks reference local landmarks from above and below — in the earlier work, filming is carried out from the ground, but by 2016 we have aerial shots via drone. MCs in these videos have adopted personas that then purport to speak from "personal experience" of a life on the outskirts. "Who's That Click" references US rap with the line "more Crips than Campton (sic)" and makes symbolic use of the colour blue, road signs and physical landmarks to signify territory and draw attention to the postcode rivalry.[24] "Promotional Hood Video" and "Who's That Click" both exhibit a youthful exuberance, showing young people enjoying life and enjoying what they do. As we arrive at the "Talks" video, however, the young men have grown up, they are more measured in their expression, they seem weary, ground down even. Despite the playfulness in some of the scenes, the spectre of death is present as one MC refers to his enemies wanting to put his face on a shirt. The message now is trust no one.

Music brings to the fore images, memories, experiences and feelings of deep attachments. According to Paul Gilroy, music as a cultural and creative practice can host "an alternative structure of feeling" where it is possible to bear the wrongs of an unjust world and maybe offer the hope of some other order, some other way of being.[25] Maybe, as Christina Sharpe asserts, creativity is an aesthetic response to the emergency of Black life in the hold. Instead of abjection, Black being embodies creativity as a form of consciousness, a survival of Black exclusion from political and cultural belonging. Performance, in this case through music, mediates survival, but more than that, it brings joy, possibility, and hope.[26] For Black youth in Newham, grime and rap music is a way to forge a sense of identity in a place deeply mired in historical and contemporary racism.

These three music videos illustrate how Black youth and young Black men have carved out room for themselves in one of the poorest areas in the UK, in an area where life chances and opportunities are limited, ever-shrinking, and informed by racism. In each video, the main MCs and the supporting chorus all play their part in leaving a trace of themselves, a legacy to be discovered at a later date. Making music allows these young men to respond to the racial terror of Black lives lived under occupation;[27] it enables them to resist, in multiple ways, the marginal roles that have been mapped out for them.

Sonically and lyrically, they place themselves at the centre of their own life stories, using wayward performing identities that, as Saidiya Hartman suggests, show value for lives that are deemed to be disposable and that refuse to conform to the privatised order of social life.[28]

To make music, young people have to come together, and make connections to the place and sounds that give them a sense of belonging. Forest Gate Youth Centre (at the corner of Dames Road and Woodgrange Road on the map) was a vibrant spot, with equipment and other resources for creative activities. After the 2008 global financial crisis and the implementation of austerity, Newham, like many areas, was forced to make cuts and, as a non-statutory service, youth provision took the biggest cut.[29] Forest Gate Youth Centre effectively became a ghost site as workers, knowledge and resources dissipated. Combined with phasing out the Education Maintenance Allowance (EMA) that provided weekly income for sixteen-nineteen year olds in Further Education[30], this made it more challenging for young people to create and share music.

Forest Gate: An Urban Village

Newham Council's Supplementary Planning Document for Forest Gate outlines its improvement plans for the area. It wants to maintain the Victorian conservation area situated in the roads off Woodgrange Road, whilst also enhancing Forest Gate as a town centre, upgrading the shopping and leisure experience and creating a relaxed "urban village" environment. The Core Strategy looks further ahead, to 2033, when "Forest Gate town centre will become an attractive and vibrant centre, retaining its urban village feel founded on established independent shops, arts and cultural activity".[31] As the town planners have also identified that the social housing estates in the roads off Woodgrange

Road are "hotspots for crime",[32] the remit of "social housing landlords" is also being extended. Social housing landlords are woven into systems that aim to address anti-social behaviour by monitoring and controlling how residents act not only within the property itself, but also in the wider neighbourbood. Overall, the council is clear that it will use its powers of enforcement, through environmental health, public order policies and legislation, "to raise the quality of the built environment" in Forest Gate town centre, which in their view has been "adversely affected by a proliferation of takeaways and betting shops... and general low levels of affluence".[33] In this new vista, cheap food for poor people is not a desirable feature.

While the new wave of gentrification may limit the possibilities of utilising public space, young Black residents continually find ways to make music that matters for them. Baseman is a rapper from Forest Gate, and his lyrics open this chapter. In his musical contribution to SBTVs Better Place series he talks about moving to Forest Gate, making specific reference to the high street and Woodgrange Road.[34] On his track, Baseman talks about relocating from another London area to Forest Gate, and about the internal conflict that underpins striving for musical excellence while simultaneously struggling with the pull of road life. Baseman asks us to consider why the location that he speaks of (and that Newham Council wants to eradicate) is known as "the Gaza". In a direct counter to Newham policymakers desire to create an "urban village", Baseman responds to the challenges faced by those who populate the location. Drawing on an old African and Caribbean sentiment of "who feels it, knows it", he asks how those who do not live there can presume to know how to deal with the difficulties that people there face. Young people in this area have been framed as troublesome, but the trouble is structural and institutional. On average, people in Newham die younger, earn less, and are more likely to be out of work, and there is a social and economic cost to these challenges.[35] For the council, one way forward in branding Newham as a desirable area is to create an urban village, populated by better off residents that do not pose a problem or add to the costs of an already stretched public purse.

Gradually, the Forest Gate area has begun to change, and an ongoing period of adjustment is in motion as the Crossrail development takes shape. The resulting work on Forest Gate Station and the redevelopment of the high street signal the arrival of the urban village. Other modifications are also visible — the children from the secondary school in Forest Lane are no longer allowed out at lunchtime, so you no longer see adolescents on the street during the daytime; a weekly market on the corner of Sebert Road offers organic foodstuffs (bread, meat, vegetables); the Railway Tavern (on the corner of Forest Lane and Woodgrange Rd on the map) becomes the Forest Tavern after a refurbishment, with folk music providing its new sonic backdrop. Slowly but surely, I come to realise that it is the young Black adults who are less visible; in many of the communal, social, or retail settings, they are missing. When I walk through Forest Gate now, I can hear music, laughter, chatter, a plethora of sounds that let me know that young Black adults are in existence, just not outside in the public arena. Those who take up space on the street are older people, and the newcomers, maybe in their late twenties, or early thirties, sometimes with small children. Their presence brings different sounds.

If you walk from Woodgrange Road along Dames Road towards Wanstead Flats, you come to a point where if you turn right you are in Redbridge, and if you turn left you are in Waltham Forest. Two different boroughs, two different approaches to policy, planning, and heritage. Place is complex, it embodies a multiplicity of cultures, meanings and identities, and this true of Newham in general and Forest Gate in particular. The composite of people, structures, institutions and social connections in this area are unfixed, subject to and influenced by policy planning.

Grime and rap both play a key role in the production of place — as a setting, the physical, built environment of the street corners, the estates, stairwells and basketball courts, and as a setting for daily social interaction — hanging out on the block. The dynamic interrelationship between music and place is disrupted if social interaction takes place mainly online or indoors. Social interaction fires the geographical imagination and allows for a sonic imagining of place. Music becomes a force that defines place, and for Black youth in Newham, it is enhanced by Black Atlantic flows that fuse together the local, the national and the global.

Conclusion

The musical choices of Black youth continue to be a source of worry and threat, and this is brought into sharp focus as east London spaces become more gentrified. Contemporary Black music such as grime, rap and UK drill feature significantly in the recent history of this location. Grime was an initially hyper-local sound, and it now has a global reach. Drill, imported from Chicago, resonated with inner-city youth, fusing its "nihilistic trap aesthetic"[36] with a distinct UK sound.

Nevertheless, making and consuming these popular musical genres is often a convivial activity among the young.[37] While rap, grime and UK drill have been cited as an incitement to gang membership, criminal activity and violence particularly amongst young Black men, I have shown how making music is a cultural, socio-economic, and political process that is resistant, enabling, and joyous.[38]

Despite gentrification, Newham as a borough remains poor. Its relatively young population has roots in the Black Diaspora and is nourished, musically at least, by its links with the Caribbean and Africa. Grime, rap, and UK drill are contemporary musical genres that support the production of local identities, but also connect to a global audience. On council estates, on street corners, in youth clubs and in schools, young people gathered to hang out and make music that mattered to them. Music that allowed them to narrate the conditions of their being, and to articulate their struggles, their joys, and their losses.

In a bid to make Newham a place where people will choose to live, work and stay, the public locations where music was made are now categorized as places of fear and deficit. The young people who occupy these spaces are rendered as troublesome and become subject to control and surveillance. It begs the question about the value placed on those who were already living, working, and staying in Newham. In their desire and aspiration for the town centre, town planners reinforce a spatial segregation along economic and cultural lines.

Historically, the high street in Forest Gate has been a site of public pleasure and entertainment. A place where people enjoyed the delights of the theatre and the cinema. Wanstead Flats, the large green space that signals the edge of Epping Forest, still hosts a funfair on bank holidays. In the roads off Woodgrange Road and in the surrounding areas on the map, young people found ways to make these areas work for them — they became territories for play and sites of creativity. Public space is free to use and when you have few resources, like the young people in Newham, a no-cost venue whether inside or outside is invaluable. Before austerity, the youth club on the corner of Dames Road and Woodgrange Road offered facilities, staff and expertise. After the cuts, very little of this was still available. Out of these meagre rations, young people made music that became a global phenomenon. Viewing these young people and the places they inhabit as objects to be feared lessens the possibility of certain musical genres being made in these places. In the prospective urban village, sanitised sounds, emitted at low volumes, erase the urgent, raucous vibrancy of grime and rap.

CHAPTER FOUR
WHY LIVE ANYWHERE ELSE?

"Our End" of Forest Gate

Forest Gate today is a highly desirable area. Wanstead Flats, the large open space at the centre of Forest Gate North, adds weight to the local council's desire to rebrand the area as an "urban village". Woodgrange Road, the high street, runs for approximately four hundred metres, with the main road at one end and the start of Wanstead Flats at the other. During the World Cup, I saw a picture on social media — England had reached the semi-final and there were celebrations everywhere. The picture showed the crowd waiting to watch the game at one of the new social venues in Forest Gate. Everyone in the picture appeared to be white. So, how is it possible, in this super diverse area of London, to create pockets of whiteness? How has it been possible to recreate, in these few streets, what seems like a reversal back to a 1970s-style separation of communities? Now, once more, it appears we have two colonies, the well-off workers (WOW), and the rest.

The leisure spots in the area are displayed on social media as supposed examples of how an area can be regenerated for the better. Customers, residents and the businesses themselves comment about how much they are able to enjoy anything, from craft beers to live Oompah:

Like seasonal beers and wines? Like German sausage and love Oompah? Well the ▮▮ and @▮▮▮▮▮▮▮ might just have something for you.

In response to a newspaper article that trotted out tired tropes of "left behind" areas and drug dealing on street corners,[1] I posed two questions on Twitter: How has having a craft beer venue under the railway arches made the area better? What makes you feel at home?

One person who responded listed many of the new venues, and said that they liked the sense of community that came with having these places to meet in. For one person, the fact that the venue had music that they liked — "Events with artists you'd never normally see in our neck of the woods" — made him travel into Forest Gate when he had "never had cause to go to FG before that".

Figure 2: Estate Agent's window stating "Why live anywhere else?" The first seven reasons to live in E7 (Forest Gate) are: Wanstead Flats, Crossrail, Westfield Shopping Centre, Clapton FC, Olympic Park, The Wanstead Tap, and the Farmers Market. A further seven reasons are: Epping Forest, Victorian terraced houses, regeneration plans, creative professionals, Familia coffee shop, thirteen minutes from the city, The Corner Kitchen (deli, pizzeria — now closed).

As well as being the site of many new leisure spaces, Woodgrange Road is also (according to the Metropolitan Police), one of the ten most crime-ridden streets in Newham.[2] When, in April 2018, a new estate agent set up in the area, it posed the question: Why live anywhere else? In their shopfront window they listed fourteen reasons why they felt Forest Gate made a great place to live. Forest Gate, in common with the rest of Newham, is a visibly multicultural area, and I was surprised to see that these aspects were excluded from the list.

Contemporary demographic change in Forest Gate is mainly due to rising house prices in the inner city, combined with a desire for urban living. People who have moved in more recently desire urban, rather than suburban living. But while there appears to be a commitment by these people to living in a diverse urban area, the different communities do not necessarily come into contact in any meaningful way.

The connections between social structures and lived experience are complex and nuanced. Somehow, the lived experiences, social spaces and social activities of the new residents of the borough have created pockets of whiteness in a mostly multicultural area. A sense of belonging in these new spaces is underpinned by community connections forged with networks that include local businesses and leisure pursuits, as well as the regulating authorities, the council and the police. Relationships are made via social media and in shared recreational spaces. Local councillors are proud of the contributions and positive attention brought to the area by new enterprise and community efforts. For example, a local Labour councillor for Forest Gate North showed her support for the businesses in the proposed urban village.[3] Here is one example from April 2018:

Happy birthday to the wonderful ████████ ...Making
our community great for 5 years today. Pop in for cake
(carrot cake is especially good), a drink, and good chat
as always.

And another from August 2018:

Pretty chuffed to see today's breakfast in the Guardian!
Bravo @████

The local police also use social media to make positive
relationships with the community in the urban village:

Such a lovely shop and an important part of the Forest
Gate Community. It would be a real sad loss to the area
should it disappear. Please have a look at their crowd
funding page.[4]

Community campaigns to improve the neighbourhood,
working in partnership with the local police, carrying
out litter patrols, reporting dumped goods, organizing
resistance to a local thoroughfare from being closed off,
and saving a local pub that has fallen into disuse enhance
a sense of pride and belonging. Although I have lived in
the area for a number of years, I had not visited many of
the venues that make Forest Gate, according to the estate
agent, a "great place to live", and I wanted to remedy that
by trying out some of the sites at various times of the day.
All of these visits were carried out in 2018.

Tales from the Field

I visited four of the locations on the estate agent's list,
making more than one visit to each venue. These are places
that I walk past on most days, on my way to the station or

to the supermarket. Since the field research, one more shop has opened, where you can use your own recycled jars to buy household produce (and have coffee). One coffee shop has closed down, but a new one has since taken its place. The deli has also closed down, unable to wait any longer for the work on the boarded-up shops to start. Taken together, these leisure locations construct a somewhat nostalgic setting — there appears to be a yearning to recreate an imagined past Britain, with handmade bread, wooden children's bicycles, a farmers market, and Wanstead Flats acting as the equivalent of the village green.

Figure 3: The artisan bakery under the railway arches selling a range of baked goods including vegan haggis sausage rolls.

At the time of writing, under another section of the railway arches, a new bakery/cafe has opened up. Set between a car mechanic and a steel fabricator, it offers, among other produce, vegan haggis sausage rolls.

In these new social spaces the multicultural nature of the area appears to be only a backdrop. Repurposed furniture and mismatched cups/cutlery in all of the leisure locations that I visited added to the sense that poverty is used as a kind of quirky exotica.

The Pub (Sunday Lunchtime)

Two of us, two Black women, occupied a window seat in the pub. Styled as a traditional pub, it is owned by a chain comprising fifty London venues. On its Twitter bio, it states that it is a "Great British Boozer, Great Ale, Great Food". Soft jazz plays. It's a child friendly venue with large garden out the back. In the heart of a multicultural high street, this space was almost exclusively white. Two West Ham football fans entered the pub wearing their colours and their football shirts. They sat down, realised their mistake and looked very uncomfortable. One of them went to the bar and ordered two pints. They drank them quickly and left. Their visit lasted less than fifteen minutes. I watched them walk out and into the pub next door (no soft jazz, no gastro food menu, "a traditional 1930s pub"). I remembered the last time I came here, several years before, when it was run by a Ghanaian couple and they had a pool table and a live reggae band. Lunch in here costs about £15.00. I noticed a sign at the bar — £2.50 for one "hand-made scotch egg". As we finished our lunch, the live band arrived.

Figure 4: Scotch eggs for sale in the gastro pub

As they set up, I wonder what type of music it would be. It was folk music. The voices, the clothes — everything signals new communities, new residents. Through the window, I watched multicultural Forest Gate walk on by.

The Deli

Four of us, two older Black women, one younger woman and a child, spent a couple of hours in this space. I was the first to arrive from our group. I sat at a table for four and explained that three more were to come. The waitress wanted me to order immediately (before I had even sat down), so I ordered something to drink. There were a few other customers. We were there for about two hours before it started to fill up. We were the only Black customers, and that did not change during our entire visit. The others arrived, but by then, the venue had more people in it so we had become invisible. We waited a long time for the menus to come back to the table (the waitress took them away even though I asked her to leave them). Everything was too much trouble. I got the strong sense that we were in the way. People came in to order takeaway pizza, and the staff were attentive and welcoming. Many of the new customers came in with children, as there was a playspace downstairs. Again the staff were hospitable and friendly to all who came in. However, when our five-year-old got out of her seat, the staff became anxious about her moving around. We ordered our food, eventually, and resigned ourselves to the lack of service. Once the food arrived, we all settled in and passed a pleasant hour or two. We asked for the bill and then I made my cultural blunder — I thought she had brought me a cup of tea, even though we were ready to leave (she hadn't, it's how they present the bill — in a teacup).

The Coffee Shop

I went here on Grand National day, a stopping-off point before I made my way to one of the betting shops in Woodgrange Road. I met my daughter there. She was in work clothes, so wearing a uniform, I was in a tracksuit. We put our bags down on a chair. Having asked my daughter what she wanted, she looked at the menu on the wall, and asked for a latte. While she was doing so, I also looked at the menu; I was being a little bit indecisive. The vibe was uncomfortable, the two white women behind the counter were irritated by our presence (maybe they wanted to lock up — it was half an hour to closing time, maybe we were taking too long). But in the end, despite the sighing and the hard faces, I asked if I could I place my order; one tea, and one latte, to drink here. Slowly, one of the women came from the back of the shop (it is quite small but it still took a her a while to get to the counter). She asked me to repeat my order (twice more), and clearly had difficulty understanding what I said. At this point, there were no other people in the cafe except me and my daughter.

After I finally placed my order she said, "Is that all?" I was being extra polite, but she rolled her eyes anyway. I looked at my daughter, we exchanged glances. I knew what to do. I said, "Please cancel the order, I've changed my mind". As she had already made the tea, I paid for it. And then we left. We were in there for less than five minutes.

The Pub 2 (Evening)

Two of us, one Black, one white, both women, went to the pub at about 8pm. The bar staff were efficient and friendly, although they were surprised when I paid for the food and drinks in cash. In the main bar, there are mismatched chairs and tables. When my chunky chips arrived (£3.30), they were served in a thick ceramic bowl. On this visit, I noticed the worn, old hardback books on the window sill, propped up by some kind of brass musical instrument.

This time there was a DJ who played a selection of soul and RnB. The music was not very loud, it was more background noise rather than the main focus. Most of the clientele stayed seated. It was a pleasant and comfortable experience but the customer base was not very diverse in terms of ethnicity. Gazing out of the window, I saw a multicultural Forest Gate community walking past as they left the station. Now, whenever I go past, I make a point of glancing into the pub window. One year on, it is still the same. The scene in the pub reflects a version of Forest Gate as a place where people live side by side, but have little contact with each other in social and community spaces.

Figure 5: Window decoration at the gastro pub with an eclectic selection of books and a brass instrument.

The Farmers Market

I worked here with a friend on her pop-up market stall on two very cold Saturdays. My friend is selling herbal teas, juices and soup. I am in charge of the soup. Long days, from

9am until 2pm. We were positioned near a shop (selling bric-a-brac) because we needed electricity for the juicer. All of this had been pre-arranged with the organiser. The pitch fee had been paid in advance some weeks prior. I watched as men and women arrived on bicycles and on foot to buy fruit, bread, meat and vegetables. People stop to have hot drinks and chat. There was a strong sense of community; some were obviously regular customers, the stallholders greeted them by name. After a few hours, while my sister went to get something out of the car, the organiser — who has been chatting to the other stallholders — comes over. She "just wanted to see how we were getting on", and "oh, by the way, have you paid for your pitch?"

In the shops adjacent to the market, I noticed that there is an African-Caribbean grocer's shop, where the owner sells similar fruit, vegetables, groceries to the farmers market, as well as African-Caribbean produce (yam, green banana, plaintain). On the two days that I worked there, there was no crossover between the market and the grocer's shop. Although they shared the same space, they had no shared customer base and limited interaction. Some days later, I was waiting at the bus stop. I noticed that the Council's Enforcement Officer was instructing the owner to remove her boxes of fruit and vegetables from outside of the shop because they were obstructing the pavement.

Why Live Anywhere Else?

Resources and power protect you from the everyday challenges of urban living. The neighbourhood can be brightened and made better with flowers, plant pots and folk music. Scaffolding and restoration work indicate an investment in property, and there is a corresponding emotional investment in the neighbourhood — the bread stall at the farmers market puts its profits into a local women's refuge. Recently, one of the shops suffered a downturn in sales because of the continuing roadworks in preparation for Crossrail. Local residents started a crowdfunder and, working together, raised more than £2,000 to help keep the business afloat.[5] In an interview with the local newspaper, it is clear that the business owner, after six years in that spot, sees himself as embedded into the community:

> The importance is that people know this is a safe place. All the kids know who I am. We always try and look after the people that are vulnerable in the area. We try to support the community the best we can.

As you walk around the neighbourhood, there are other examples of emotional investment in the Forest Gate community that exist beyond the highly visible leisure spaces: jumble trails where people can set up a stall outside of their home, street parties, festivals, and fundraising for local causes. The paradox though is that the capacity to do this is built on structural inequalities that enable the new residents to be able to afford to buy or rent homes in Newham and have the capacity to engage in civic participation. Identities, as young couples, as young parents with particular tastes and interests, are forged in the social and leisure spaces. Older, established communities have developed a sense of belonging through kinship, recreation, and work.

Even those that feel at home in these new spaces are sounding a note of caution and expressing unease. Work on Crossrail is still not completed, with the opening date pushed back time and again. In the high street, shops earmarked for demolition have been boarded up for many months, and building work has not yet started on the planned supermarket.

Since a car ploughed into it two years previously, one estate agent's office on Woodgrange Road has been covered in plywood and flyposting.[6] A computer repair shop opposite Forest Gate Station remains out of use after an electrical fire some months back. The boards, the peeling posters, supplemented by roadworks that cause traffic congestion in the high street, throw some doubt on whether Forest Gate is great place to live. Social media commentary, and campaigns to support businesses suffering a downturn, reflect this unease.

Figure 6: Boarded-up shops in the High Street, awaiting redevelopment into a supermarket. At the time of writing the shops had been empty for nine months

A Sense of Belonging

According to Ole Jensen and Ben Gidley, for the last two hundred years, the city has been defined by large numbers of people living close together, underpinned by pockets of difference.[7] By 1965, new legislation meant that mass migration from former colonies like Jamaica had ended. And by 1971, this meant that the main countries of origin for immigrants to the UK were Ireland, India, Jamaica and Pakistan. In the mid-1970s, the displacement of east African Asians from Kenya and Uganda ushered in a new wave of migration.[8] These communities are represented in Newham, and in Forest Gate, along with those from Eastern Europe.[9] Globalisation, poverty, and conflict in the Global South have heightened the push factors for movement to the UK — for example, in the 1980s and 1990s, there were more asylum applications from Zimbabwe, Somalia, Eritrea, and Sudan.[10]

In many cities in the UK, the experience of different cultural groups living side by side is a fairly typical one. In Forest Gate, it is possible to see how that difference is accommodated and/or ignored. For Stuart Hall, the questions here are about how groups that are different in terms of their cultural, religious, linguistic, and historical backgrounds can co-exist, but I would add that economic background is also significant here. How is it possible, Hall asks, for these different groups to occupy the same spaces "without either group hating one another"?[11]

For the new residents, their communities and identities have been created online and offline. Social media (Twitter in particular) shows support for certain kinds of local business and leisure activities, and in so doing, amplifies place-based identities in what some people describe as "our end" of Forest Gate. References are made to the postcode and with the hashtag #ForestGate. Campaigning — for example to stop a thoroughfare being closed off, or to prevent further dereliction of a listed building — also supports the development of a sense of belonging. And of course, individual acts from the WOW community do this too, for example highlighting on social media obvious signs of poverty such as homes in disrepair, or anti-social behaviour such as flytipping. While there was a cycle ride in support of a young man who had been stabbed to death near Sebert Road,[12] there was no campaign and very little commentary on two recent separate shooting incidents — in the first of which a fourteen-year-old schoolboy died, and the second when a twenty-five-year-old man was left with "lifechanging injuries" within the vicinity of "our end of Forest Gate".

For the WOW residents with young children, activities in community and commercial spaces also create a sense of belonging, from indoor playspaces in local eateries to Saturday morning ballet classes in a nearby community centre. Sublocal identities are formed through leisure pursuits, and social groupings allow WOW residents to live their imagined "urban village" life. Whether inadvertent or deliberate, disparities in economic and social capital facilitate a closing off of diversity. According to Gidley, Hanson and Ali, sublocal, place-based identities "feed into and emerge from the efforts of the state".[13] In Forest Gate, those efforts are made via the Local Development Plan, but in its drive to create an "urban village" little room is left for different groups to interact in community spaces as young Black residents are corralled into ever decreasing areas.

In *New Urban Multicultures*, sociologist Les Back argues that it is not simply the type of space available, but how people use it, that has an impact on place-based identities and belonging. In the inner city, in places like Forest Gate, people live with difference in a way that can be categorised as "separate together". Communities need opportunities to come together and interact, and this can happen in public spaces such as markets or parks.

At the weekly farmers market, shoppers that feel a sense of belonging (and who can afford to buy the produce) stop and buy, the rest walk on, while existing stores such as the African-Caribbean grocer are monitored and policed. Without sites where different communities can interact, the possibilities for social cohesion are limited. If the focus of interaction is based around consumption then, according to Les Back, it promotes "superficial mixing in some groups".[14] A multitude of sites would offer opportunities for deeper, more meaningful interactions, thereby increasing the chances of a more cohesive community. Forest Gate as a neighbourhood is not unlike many UK cities where socio-economic segregation is becoming more ingrained than ethnic segregation.[15]

In these environments, wealth is not necessarily displayed in an ostentatious manner. There are instead a number of sophisticated and subtle ways to convey status, including being able to buy property at a price that is beyond the reach of most residents, as well as the social performances of leisure pursuits, like attending ballet class or dining in the gastropub.

Gentrification has been repackaged as regeneration, and it occurs at sites of previous national and local disinvestment. As a process, one feature of gentrification is residential reformation, however a complex economic, social and spatial restructuring is also at work here. Transformation of the social environment is highly desired by Newham policymakers and planners. Kate Shaw argues that in these regenerated spaces, we can see a generalised middle-class restructuring of place that results in the displacement of those without the economic or political power to resist.[16] Tactics of bio-power and discipline underpinned by policy and planning initiatives mean that for young Black adults in poor communities, social housing estates effectively become sites of monitoring, surveillance, and curtailment, whilst WOW communities are not subject to the disciplining of leisure activities or public space in the same way. These mechanisms create different forms of displacement, which Tom Slater urges us to "document from below, in the sobering terms of those who experience it".[17]

It would appear there are many drivers for the middle classes to seek to relocate in previously disinvested neighbourhoods and it would seem that there is a desire to be at home in the urban rather than the suburban environment. We can see this in the way that WOW communities invest their social, cultural and economic capital in areas previously considered to be "risky" by investors and estate agents. What is less clear is *why* they want to invest in territorially stigmatised areas and then try to create sublocales with a distinct place-identity that appears to be at odds with what is already there. WOW communities use aesthetic strategies to distinguish themselves from existing less well-resourced communities. These social distinctions play out on the streets, in the aesthetics of the bottle-green or grey woodwork, and in the scaffolding for the loft conversion that soon follows the removal of the estate agent's "Sold" sign.

Cities have become increasingly polarised, with a sharper divide between the wealthy and the poor. By focussing on a hyper-local demarcation in Forest Gate, we can see how working-class consumption and leisure pursuits in a disadvantaged area are gradually being replaced by more prosperous forms. The drive from the council's regeneration programme to create an urban village, with bars, cafes, and creative/cultural outlets, flattens existing consumption and makes undesirable the consumer options that already existed there, including takeaways and cheap fruit and vegetables at £1 a bowl.

Research shows that even in ethnically and socially mixed neighbourhoods, the better off live in their own enclave; school choices, leisure choices, and work habits maintain social segregation.[18] Access to resources limits choices, not just in leisure but also in essentials such as housing. If access to leisure is through consumption, there are very few places that you can go into if you have little or no money, especially if one of the cheapest items in the pub is a scotch egg for £2.50.

As we saw in Chapter Three, young people might stake their claim to an area through music, by referencing particular places in their lyrics and in their videos. This is also done by using graffiti to physically mark the territory, or maybe even by hanging out in a particular public spot. Just along from the artisan bakery under the railway arches, where the vegan haggis sausage rolls are for sale, it is possible to see names, initials, and the postcode E7 etched into a paving stone, just about visible.

Now however, in a newly gentrified Forest Gate, Black youth and young Black adults have become folk devils in terms of crime and anti-social behaviour. In many ways, group-specific behaviour produces space, and reproduces identities. The carefully positioned flower beds and edible gardens brighten the area, but also send a clear message about who belongs, especially if they are literally embedded in the street furniture installed to act as a deterrent to stop people gathering.

Despite the slowdown in building work, and the delays with Crossrail, the town planners' dream of a multicultural urban village in Forest Gate is taking shape. Old and new migration histories are transmitted through the leisure activities and consumption patterns. Some stories are highly visible, others are becoming less so. A sense of belonging is nourished by shared activities, but when the entry to those activities depends on your ability to purchase, we can see how in an area with sharp inequalities in income, those who are well off flock together. On the whole, the wealthier residents are removed from the daily realities of the urban poor.

Figure 7: Paving slab in E7, a few steps away for the artisan bakery under the railway arches. E7 is referenced, and the young people have carved their names into the stone; Jess, Jamie, Louis, Kyle and Antony.

The city, or in this case the hyper-local demarcation of one square mile in Forest Gate, illustrates spatial expressions of inequality. Maybe Forest Gate really is a world cut in two, a world divided by access to resources. However, the challenge is how to resist social and economic segregation in a place where belonging is selective and communities live separately, side by side.

CHAPTER FIVE
WINS AND LOSSES

What was Forest Gate like in 1974?

Well, school was quite mixed, many Black faces, but mainly white. Not as many Asians as there are now. Outside, it wasn't a friendly place, people didn't mind telling you to your face that you were a Black this and a Black that... there was a sense of entitlement from the older white people. I remember once, I was about 16, I think, being shoved out of the way at the bus stop, saying something to the effect that she should go before me because her husband was in the war.

— Paulette, 57[1]

It was alright, Newham was always alright, there was tension between people, Asian, Black and white, but we could still banter, especially if we were working together. But if you were on the street, and people were attacking you, that's different...

— Winston, 63[2]

Three Incidents: Forest Gate Now

On the map, there are three exclamation marks, each indicating an incident where gunshots were fired: the first is at Clare Gardens, the second at Brooking Road, and the final one at Dames Road. One incident happened during the daytime, the other two occurred at night. In total, one person died and one person was seriously injured. Three arrests were made.

Incident 1: April 2017, Clare Gardens

An unnamed twenty-five-year-old man is shot at, he survives. It is reported in the local paper only, but not featured on the local or national news.[3]

Incident 2: September 2017, Brooking Road

Corey Junior Davis, known as CJ, was fourteen years old when he died after being shot in the head.[4] I remember walking home from Forest Gate Station on that day. More people than usual were gathered in the street. I heard snatches of conversation as I walked through the crowd, gunshots were mentioned.

Incident 3: July 2018, Dames Road

The final point on an armed police chase that started a few miles away in Leytonstone. Armed police open fire at the vehicle, shooting out the back window. The car comes to its final stop in Dames Road.

The Clare Gardens episode attracted local coverage only; it took place in the context of many other incidents, everyday acts that go unnoticed and unremarked. Here, a young man was left with lifechanging injuries. The newspaper gives no details of the injuries, but being on the receiving end of them must impact on your emotional well-being as well as physical health. What does it *feel* like to survive being shot? If others were present, it must leave a mark on them to have witnessed such an event. The story of CJ, the fourteen-year-old-boy who died in the second incident, because he was so young, made the national media. A Serious Case Review of the events leading up to his death makes sober reading. A schoolboy, sitting with his friend on a wall, passing the time, is murdered in broad daylight. What does it *feel* like to be at someone's side when their life is ending? When the police fire shots in residential streets as they chase a car late at night, the possibility of collateral damage looms, and anxiety hangs in the air. I was in the crowd that gathered on the night of the third incident — shock, fear and a sense of the inevitable hung in the air. I could hear people speculating whether the young men were dead, because there was no ambulance on the scene. There were maybe fifty or so of us watching the events unfold on that summer evening, all trying to understand what had happened. Hearing the sirens and the helicopter overhead for hours afterwards, disrupts the senses in a deeply visceral way.

Figure 8: 28th July 2018 shooting in Forest Gate. On the scene are armed response vehicles (ARVs), twelve officers are visible, there are at least another thirty outside of the frame.

A Hostile Environment

During a five-week period in 2017, four Black men died after being restrained by the police. On 15th June, twenty-five-year-old Edir Frederico Da Costa, known as Edson, was stopped by the Metropolitan Police in Beckton, in the south of the London Borough of Newham. He was restrained, handcuffed and sprayed with CS gas. Unconscious, he was taken to hospital. He died six days later on 21st June.[5] Suspected of robbery, Shane Bryant was arrested in Ashby-de-la-Zouch on 14th July. Shane was "taken ill" during the arrest, and died two days later. Darren Cumberbatch, a thirty-two-year-old man from Nuneaton died on the 19th July. After being tasered, pepper sprayed and restrained by the police he "became unwell" and was taken to a nearby hospital where he died. On 22nd July, Rashan Charles, a twenty-year-old, was chased by the police into a shop in Dalston. Rashan was subsequently pinned down and restrained by a Metropolitan Police officer; one hour later he was dead.[6]

When Edson died, people took to the streets to protest. Starting with a rally in Stratford, on the 26th June, the procession walked the mile or so to Forest Gate police station. Picture if you will some of the scenes on social media and in the mainstream media. The protest was loud but uneventful at first. Later on in the evening, young people came into direct contact with the police and they clashed.[7] On a Channel 4 news report, Woodgrange Rd, the high street at the heart of the urban village, is clearly visible.[8] We can see how police, dressed in riot gear, form a hard border across Woodgrange Road, using dogs and weapons in response to relatively minor incidents. Small fires are started, fireworks and some missiles are thrown.

When we consider these recent events, and the institutional response to community protest, it reinforces the notion that, in the UK, Black communities have always existed in a hostile environment. Although it might appear that the hostile environment promoted by Home Secretary Theresa May was a recent policy, in fact it has been in operation almost since the arrival of the post-war Commonwealth migrants. The 1962 Commonwealth Immigrants Act was the start of a decades-long process of restricted entry, audit and surveillance of Black populations that continues to this day. The Labour Party, led by James Callaghan, continued this anti-immigration stance, and in 1968 rushed through a second Commonwealth Immigrants Act to stop Kenyan Asians from entering Britain.[9] The 1971 Immigration Act stopped all primary Black immigration. "Patrials", a code word for the people from the white Commonwealth (New Zealand and Australia) were unaffected.[10] Noting that the law was about to change, Black adults stayed put and sent for their children while they still had access to citizenship.

In a television interview in 1978, Margaret Thatcher spoke out about immigration and unemployment. In response to a question about why a reduction to immigration would be policy if the Conservatives got into power, she had this to say:

I think it means that people are really rather afraid that this country might be rather swamped by people with a different culture and, you know, the British character has done so much for democracy, for law and done so much throughout the world that if there is any fear that it might be swamped people are going to react and be rather hostile to those coming in.

It is not as if we have great wide open spaces or great natural resources; we have not. So, either you go on taking in 40 or 50,000 a year, which is far too many, or you say we must hold out the prospect of a clear end to immigration and that is the view we have taken and I am certain that is the right view to keep good race relations and to keep fundamental British characteristics which have done so much for the world.[11]

Her words regarding the "British character... that has done so much for law and throughout the world" make no reference to the violence and terror of Britain's imperialist and colonial past, nor offer any recognition of how Britain has benefited from Black labour or its contribution to Britain's economic wealth. By suggesting that Britain was being "swamped", Thatcher's words framed Black people as a threat and legitimised hostility against Black populations.

In a hostile, virulently anti-Black environment, groups of migrants formed bonds that transcended islands and ethnic groupings to continue anti-racist and anti-colonial struggles. For example, anti-racist campaigns were organised to deal with racism in the workplace and in social situations.[12] This became what Sivanandan called a "mosaic of unities" that formulated itself into a "shifting pattern of Black unity and Black struggle".[13] The perceived end of empire underpinned by an ideology of racial superiority drove a push towards the re-formation of racist organisations: the British Union of Fascists, the White Defence League, and the British National Party, for example, who took their racial violence to the street. In 1959 in Notting Hill, which had a large Caribbean population, Kelso Cochrane was stabbed to death by an unidentified white youth. In 1967, the League of Empire Loyalists and the British National Party merged to form the National Front. Post his 1968 "Rivers of Blood" speech, Enoch Powell called for repatriation (voluntary but encouraged, for Black migrants).[14] In Newham, crosses were burned outside "coloured citizens homes" in Plaistow.[15] Despite his verbal opposition to Enoch Powell's ideas, Edward Heath, the Conservative Prime Minister, opted to push through legislation that severely restricted immigration.

These changes in legislation meant that settlement and/or citizenship was contingent and could be removed. The 1981 British Nationality Act introduced the good character test, and excluded certain Commonwealth identities from nationality. Adults with Leave to Remain in the UK are non-citizens, and their children (even if born in the UK) are non-citizens. For foreign nationals, powers already existed to deport and exclude them, but this legislation cleared the way for removals and deportations even for UK-born adults.[16] Deportations of the Windrush Generation highlight these policies in practice.[17] In addition, the implementation of the Nationality, Immigration and Asylum Act 2002 and the Immigration, Asylum and Nationality Act 2006 meant that dual nationals with British citizenship could be deprived of their citizenship. The Nationality, Immigration and Asylum Act 2002 also meant that naturalized Britons could have their British nationality removed and effectively be made stateless if it was thought that they could acquire citizenship elsewhere.

For some politicians, the hostile environment did not go far enough. According to David Cameron there was a "a gap in our armoury" for dealing with citizens born and raised in Britain who did not possess another nationality.[18] With the Immigration Act 2014 it became possible to remove passports and issue temporary exclusion orders ostensibly as a response to terrorist threat. According to Kapoor and Narkowic, the power to remove passports had been in place for decades, but

The provisions were enhanced significantly, however, when they were updated in April 2013, and set out in a Written Ministerial Statement by Theresa May

(2013). The revised policy established that there was "no entitlement to a passport and no statutory right to have access to a passport" (May 2013) and reconfirmed that the "decision to issue, withdraw or refuse a passport" was at the discretion of the Home Secretary.[19]

Theresa May stated that the enforcement of this measure was to be used sparingly. It had to be necessary, proportionate and in the public interest to do so. However, the "public interest" criteria for refusing or withdrawing a passport was redefined. The new criteria of assessment would account for a person's "past, present or proposed activities".[20] All of this leaves people open to loss of citizenship and/or deportation on vague and spurious grounds.

Policing

In terms of policing, everyday acts of racism are a fact of life for Black communities. In the 1970s and 1980s, "sus" laws and Stop and Search actions were used frequently against Black youth. Police harassment of Black youth on the street was a familiar strategy as Black people were seen as deviant by nature, and policed accordingly. In 1982, Kenneth Newman, the Metropolitan Chief of Police, is reported to have said:

In the Jamaicans, you have people who are constitutionally disorderly... It's simply in their make-up. Jamaicans are...constitutionally disposed to be anti-authority.[21]

From the 1970s on, there was a steady deterioration in the relationship between Black youth and the police. The "sus" laws mentioned above derived from the Vagrancy Act 1824, and were used to stop and search youth on the street. "Sus" allowed any person that the police believed to be acting suspiciously to be stopped, searched and possibly arrested. Many of these searches, including body searches, took place in public. "Sus" was abandoned in 1981 after nationwide inner-city civil disturbances. The Police and Criminal Evidence Act 1984 was introduced to provide a clear framework for stop and search, detention and arrest.[22]

The Special Patrol Group (SPG) was set up as an elite division of the London Metropolitan Police. Taking its name from the counter terrorism unit in Northern Ireland, its officers were specially trained to neutralise trouble spots.[23] A centrally based, mobile unit, it operated from 1961 to 1987, and could be deployed to deal with serious public disorder in any area. Although it was a uniformed division, many of the officers worked in plain clothes. SPG had a notorious reputation and were renowned for using high levels of violence. Robert Mark, the Chief Commissioner for the Metropolitan Police at the time, wrote the following in his autobiography:

> Some of the tactics adopted by the London police ... were those developed and used by the army and the RUC SPG [Royal Ulster Constabulary — Special Patrol Group] in Northern Ireland. The introduction of "snatch squads" and "wedges" in demonstrations, and random stop and searches and roadblocks on the streets were based on the Army's experience in Ulster.[24]

I spoke to Winston, a sixty-three-year-old Black man of Caribbean descent and a long-term Newham resident. Winston recalled his encounters with the police generally, and the SPG in particular, in the 1980s as follows:

> They would abuse you, call you names, they would try and trigger something in you to start something so they can arrest you. They would taunt you and say derogatory

things. If you look at most people from back then, I think 70% of the youth growing up back then would have assault on police on their records.

And on the SPG he had this to say:

In them days, they were like savages. We went to the police station because they had arrested my mum, and my aunt. We weren't allowed to leave, they locked the door, SPG came from around the back and started throwing punches.

The SPG were trained to use military techniques that included a show of force and sonic warfare. Controversy followed them, and a notorious incident involved the death of Blair Peach, a teacher and anti-racist campaigner who took part in an Anti-Nazi League rally in 1979. During the protest, Blair Peach was struck on the head and later died from his injuries.[25]

Civil Unrest and Uprising

Nationally, 1981 was a watershed year for inner-city Black youth. Even though the whole country experienced deep economic recession, for Caribbean youth unemployment levels were disproportionately high. The offspring of Caribbean migrants, whether born in Britain or not, were in the UK to stay. Black youth had been demonised as criminals or at the very least as having a propensity to crime. Certain crimes were racialised as "black". Street robbery, positioned as "mugging", had become a moral panic.[26]

In January 1981, thirteen Black teenagers died in a house fire in New Cross, in what was believed to be a racially-motivated arson attack.[27] In nearby Brixton in the same year, against a backdrop of rising crime, the Metropolitan Police extended its application of sus and increased its stop and search activities. In April, in an operation known as "Swamp 81", the number of uniformed officers patrolling the street was increased. As well as additional officers from other police districts, the SPG was deployed into Brixton. Over a five-day period, almost 950 people were stopped and searched and 82 were arrested. By day five, Brixton was in flames. Unrest spread to other areas, and between April and July that year there were many uprisings, the most serious being in Birmingham, Leeds and Liverpool.

Policing was one part of a complex landscape underpinned by economic and social inequality, issues of identity, and grounded in the racism that Black British youth came up against. As a response to the riots, the Conservative government commissioned a QC, Robert Scarman, to investigate causes and concerns. In his report, Scarman saw firsthand the plight of Black youth in the UK in term of inequality, housing, and access to jobs and training.

A Hostile Environment in Newham

As a counter resistance to the hostile environment of the 1980s, the Newham Monitoring Project was formed in 1980. Based in Forest Gate, it formed part of a community campaign after a teenager, Akhtar Ali Baig, was murdered in Newham by a racist skinhead gang. Starting out as an organisation that monitored council and police responses to racist attacks, its brief soon extended to the investigation of police misconduct. According to the NMP, in 1985, a National Demonstration Against Racism was held in Newham after the police used "snatch squads" against protestors outside Forest Gate police station.

An example of the hostile environment in Newham is the case of the "First Avenue 11". In 1983, one member of the Ramsay family was followed to his home in Manor Park by a police van and helicopter. The SPG entered the house by force and arrested eleven people, all Black. They were taken to Forest Gate Police station and subsequently charged with various offences. The Newham Monitoring Project, along with two other east London community organisations, campaigned on the group's behalf and subsequently a press conference calling for an investigation into the activities of Forest Gate police was held in the House of Commons.[28]

Another example is the Pryce family. In 1984, sixteen-year-old Eustace Pryce and his older brother Gerald were involved in a fight with a group of white youths. Eustace was stabbed in the head and died outside the Greengate pub in Plaistow. The attack was witnessed by two plain clothes police officers, who saw the incident from the top of a passing double decker bus. Once they arrived at the scene, the police arrested Gerald and let the white youths go. Gerald Pryce was charged with affray and remanded in custody. Afterwards, Martin Newhouse, who struck the fatal blow, was arrested and charged with the murder of Eustace Pryce.[29] Newhouse was granted bail to allow him to celebrate Christmas with his family. Gerald Pryce on the other hand remained in custody, and when he was eventually released on bail, the bail conditions kept him out of Newham and away from his family.

Housing, Work and Education

Although the post-war wave of migration from the Caribbean was on the wane by 1955, anti-Black sentiment was entrenched in the UK. Housing was a fiercely contested site, and Black migrants were, on the whole, living in poor quality houses of multi-occupation. Newham, like many areas with a post-war migrant population, experienced a racial division of labour, housing and leisure. Collective and individual action from Caribbean and Asian migrants came in the form of campaigns, protests, and publications, as well as setting up organisations such as supplementary schools.[30] The lack of access to decent housing for rent led to Asian and Caribbean communities pooling their savings so that they could buy property together. For example, the Jamaican system of "pardner" and the Trinidadian system of "sou-sou" were informal loan systems where people pooled their money and took it in turns to have a loan, which was often used as a foundation to buy property.[31] In Newham, this was mainly in the north of the borough, including Forest Gate. In some areas, this prompted further anger from the white population, who felt that their homes and livelihoods were being taken away.[32] The fear of losing a "traditional Britain", with jobs being taken by foreigners, saw many politicians fight on a racist ticket — in Birmingham, for example, "If you want a nigger for a neighbour, vote Labour" was used as a political campaign slogan.[33]

As communities became more settled, British-born children and those from the Caribbean took up their places in school. For children of Caribbean heritage, racism in education was framed in terms of behavioural difficulties, poor language skills, and children who were often classified as educationally sub-normal and placed in separate schools.[34]

Contemporary Newham

According to 2011 census data, Forest Gate is categorised as "Multicultural Metropolitan: Inner City" by the Office of National Statistics.[35] Newham is a historically poor borough that has experienced the worst effects of forty years of neoliberalism and a decade of austerity. It is a toxic mix. With cuts to services, Newham lost the majority of its youth centres, whilst social services and health services have been outsourced (see Chapter Two). Newham has a great demand for social housing — according to research carried out by housing charity Shelter, Newham has the highest number of homeless people in England — 14,500 are in temporary accommodation. Shelter also counted 76 rough sleepers.[36]

On its website where potential tenants bid for property, the council makes it clear that most people will never be allocated social housing:

> Demand for social housing is extremely high in Newham and there are currently thousands of households on our housing register. The majority of people who apply will never be housed.[37]

In contemporary Newham, serious crime appears to be on the rise. In January 2018, two of Newham's top ten crime hotspots were in Forest Gate (Romford Road, at the Forest Gate end slightly out of the area I am looking at, and Woodgrange Road).[38] According to a recent report from Community Links, in 2016 Newham had more murders and more gun crime that any other London borough.[39] The council's first ever Crime and Antisocial Behaviour Scrutiny Commission heard that detectives launched thirteen murder investigations in the borough in the twelve months up to March 2018. In November 2018, the local papers reported that "Newham had the highest number of murders in London in the last year".[40] But despite these statistics, Detective Superintendent Marshall stated that the figures were now dropping — "We haven't seen a youth murder since April which is really significant".[41]

All crime, serious or minor, has an impact on victims, offenders, families and communities. As of June 2018, 786 Newham residents were held in prisons, young offender institutions and immigration removal centres in England

and Wales (see Appendix 2 — Freedom of Information (FOI) Request). This represents about 1% of the prison estate. Additionally, 1,026 of Newham residents are on probation, the majority of which are men under the age of thirty-five, and just under 50% are Black or from an ethnic minority. Each custodial sentence, each probation intervention means a rupture from family, friends, and community.

In 2014, the London Borough of Newham was twelfth highest for gang violence in London and seventh highest for serious youth violence incidents.[42] In a bid to combat youth crime in the area, Newham has made extensive use of the gangs matrix, as well as other legislation and policy measures. The gangs matrix came into being as a response to the August 2011 civil disturbances.[43] According to the Amnesty Report, the gangs matrix has an over-representation of black and ethnic minorities.[44] Controversy continues with this measure — there are issues with how individuals are added, how they can be removed, and the way that the data is stored.[45] In Newham, further issues arose when, in January 2017, the gang matrix was leaked online, and shared on social media.[46] Corey Junior Davis, the fourteen-year-old who was shot and killed in Forest Gate in September 2017, appeared on that list, and while there is no suggestion that this had anything to do with his death, a number of young people in the borough *were* put at risk. It has to be said that the "gang" narrative has become highly racialised. Claire Alexander argues that the term "gang" is being misused by the media, politicians and policymakers to reinforce its association with race and particularly African/Caribbean communities.[47]

Risk assessment is also used as a way to maintain public order, and young people are often on the receiving end of policy initiatives and processes to tackle public safety issues. Labelling groups of Black people who gather to socialise or hang out as troublesome or problematic offers easy access into the criminal justice system. In Newham, during the London 2012 Olympics, the council recruited a member of staff to vet grime and rap music videos on YouTube, and any that were deemed to have "gang" references were removed.

Young, in Newham and Black

The three incidents at the start of the chapter remind us that serious violence is never far from the surface in Forest Gate, even in the urban village. We have to place this violence in the context of a hostile environment created and maintained by successive governments, held in place by individual fears and state institutions. At the time of writing no one has been charged for shooting the unnamed twenty-five-year-old man. We will never know what effect it had on his life. CJ, the fourteen-year-old schoolboy, had come into contact with more than a dozen agencies that were supposed to protect him. He died, and the friend who was with him has to live with the trauma of what he witnessed. Despite extensive national media coverage, no arrests have been made. In the last incident, no one died, and there were no reported injuries. The shots fired were discharged by the police only, however the young men who were arrested after the chase got lengthy sentences, terms that are longer than the time they had been alive.[48] These events, combined with the deaths of four young Black men in police custody over a five-week period in Summer 2017, depict a challenging landscape for young Black lives in the inner city.

Violence to Black lives occurs against a backdrop of five decades of a hostile environment that has erased and ignored the contribution that Black citizens have made. Instead, Black communities have been positioned as a drain on British society and a danger to British norms and British values.

In 1978, Margaret Thatcher brought fears about immigration into the spotlight . Using an interview on primetime television to situate the Black presence in Britain as alien and unwanted, Thatcher normalised the language of the far right. At the same time, extreme right-wing groups like the BNP and the National Front were using street-level violence as well as the political process to further their goals. In Newham, these groups had some of their best successes, working with unions and gaining seats on the local council.

Once mass migration from the Caribbean had begun, it wasn't long before movement was severely limited by the introduction of the 1962 Commonwealth Immigrants Act. Black citizens, invited to come and use their labour to help to rebuild the "mother country", were coming home. They came for a better life, and to be in a better place. However, in Newham, violence became part and parcel of the everyday landscape, as Asian and Caribbean communities were subject to physical violence. As a result, anti-racist struggles at this time were a joint effort, with Asian and Caribbean groups setting up community organisations, campaigning and resisting racism. Children especially were targeted — "paki bashing" and "nigger hunting" occurred in schools as well as on the street, with little protection from the school system or the police.[49] Police work is by consent to maintain the peace and for the protection of the public. In the 1970s and 1980s, unhindered by Race Relations legislation, police action in Black communities was by coercion, using excessive violence and targeted harassment. Using tactics devised for paramilitary action in Northern Ireland, the Metropolitan Police, supported by its elite "third force" the SPG, used snatch squads and sonic warfare against Black youth.

Civil unrest in 1981 highlighted issues of police brutality and high unemployment for Black youth who were barely getting by, with little work, underpinned by a poor quality education. Added to this was the hostile environment, including daily microaggressions such as the events that Paulette reflects on at the start of the chapter. I have mentioned the First Avenue 11 and the campaign by the Pryce family after their son was murdered — these incidents, and many more, unreported and unspoken, are in living memory. School was not a safe haven, it repeated the behaviours and processes of life outside.

After 1981, purposeful and determined anti-racist campaigning saw local councils begin to introduce equal opportunities policies. Often, especially in poor areas, the council is a major employer. This was true of Newham, and the council had very few Black staff at the time. Like many other local authorities in the mid-1980s, however, Newham council became an equal opportunities employer, opening up job opportunities to its wider community. But this is against a backdrop of a government agenda to reduce the role of the state. After the global financial crisis in 2008, many public services (and jobs) were outsourced, and budget cuts were even more savage.

Life in Newham is precarious, even for those who thought they were citizens because they came to the country as British subjects. The threat of removal, for them and Black migrants that came in later waves, is never far from the surface. Living with uncertainty regarding your status brings anxiety about coming into contact with regulating authorities in any way. What the Windrush scandal has made visible is that citizenship can be revoked and people can be removed at any time. Even if they have broken no laws. In a further move, British-born offspring are also subject to the same limitations. Coming into contact with the criminal justice system may well end in deportation.

Against a backdrop of low wages and insecure, zero-hour contracts, the costs to apply for naturalisation (and its precursor, Indefinite Leave to Remain) are prohibitive. Therefore, for some communities in Newham, life is a perpetual state of anxiety. In a heartbeat, life could change for the worse and spin out of control. If your status can be checked or challenged, how do you ever feel at ease? How do you ever feel at home?

For some, Newham is a place of possibility, the chance of a good home at a reasonable price. A place where schools can be improved with parental participation, good governance and citizenship. But the three gun incidents at heart of the urban village tell us something about how life is lived in the less well-padded part of town. What does it feel like to be young in Newham and Black, embodying the weight of all that has gone before? Each generation is supposed to do better than the last, but it is a challenge to move to independence when social housing is non-existent, and even if you have a job, private renting and buying is out of financial reach. You can work, pay taxes and get deported. You can come into contact with the police for any reason, have your status checked, and be deported. For some young people, there is nothing to win and nothing to lose, it is a zero-sum game. Sizeable numbers of young Black Newham residents are in prison, in young offender institutions, in immigration removal centres, or on probation. Each person in this carceral system represents a loss, to a family, to a friendship group. Each time there is an incident, reported in the media or otherwise, anxiety is heightened, especially for those who belong to the less well-off part of town.

Being in the heart of a hostile environment brings fear, feelings of tension and anxiety. Everyday encounters and activities are fraught with danger and microaggressions. The Forest Gate of the past that Paulette describes in her interview may have changed on the surface, and it may seem to be a more friendly place. What we can see, however, is that socio-economic, legislative and policy mechanisms are still at work, operating as technologies of control on young Black lives.

CHAPTER SIX
IN MEMORIAM: NICO ESSIAN RAMSAY

But the dead never stop talking and sometimes the living hear.

— Marlon James, *A Brief History of Seven Killings*

The living owe it to those who no longer can speak to tell their story for them.

— Czesław Miłosz, *The Issa Valley*

When it comes to crime, serious violence is nothing new, although the choice of weapon may change over time, from belt buckles to acid to knives.[1] Violence is a deeply embedded societal issue, but individual actions plainly have consequences. Deaths and stabbings on London streets appear to be a mounting problem, particularly for the young.[2] Media in its various forms presents story after story, often invoking fear and terror, sometimes supporting campaigns for a solution. Fear of crime makes people wary and anxious. In response to news reports and social media posts the public calls for more police, increased stop and search, to lock up more people and give them longer sentences.[3] Brutal responses to crime form part of a continuum where witnessing various levels of violence becomes familiar.[4]

The societal conditions that make serious youth violence such a real possibility are embedded in at least four decades of enduring inequalities. But the issues around youth violence are often misidentified and framed out of context. The problem is not simply with youth violence — violence on the whole runs through our communities. It occurs in domestic life, at work and at play, in public and private institutions. Children and young people are on the receiving end, and they also bear witness to it. Violence is both physical and verbal, gradually permeating everyday experiences until it becomes a sickness, a form of social and emotional suffering. When combined with processes and techniques that make poverty and racism not just possible, but acceptable, maybe we do arrive at a point where for some, life — even their own — has little value.

The austerity agenda has clearly fuelled a rise in poverty, as well as physical and mental ill-health.[5] At the same time, austerity measures cut and reshaped the public sector and social services — there are no longer safety nets for people who are struggling. Prevention really is better than enforcement; the costs when a life is ended or irreparably damaged are too great. Intentionally or not, we misidentify the issues as a problem purely with Black youth and Black musical forms. It is UK drill that is now at the forefront of the problem now, previously it was grime, and prior to that it was "gangsta" rap. As we stay appalled by the content of music that is not to our taste, we miss the opportunity to hear what is going on for *some* young people. Cycles of retaliation and revenge are amplified at lightning speed through social media. When we misread the social challenges of mental health and wellbeing, school exclusion, poverty, and unemployment, we miss the opportunity to tackle the root causes. Like "mugging" before it, "knife crime" has become a Black crime even though the data suggests otherwise.[6] I have shown in previous chapters how decades of a hostile environment has produced vulnerability in young Black lives. Most crime is motivated by proximity and opportunity. In a location where the demographic is largely made up of those who are young and Black, harm will likely come from someone who looks like them, and the ultimate harm is death.

Forest Gate

As a longstanding resident, I walk through Forest Gate on most days. When I go to Woodgrange Road, or to the train station, I am in the heart of the proposed urban village. Although, if you tread through the streets of your city with a young Black man, you see the world differently. Young Black men are hyper-visible, as they come up against everyday surveillance, and they are hyper-vigilant in an attempt to pre-empt any situation that might take on a tricky turn. My nineteen-year-old nephew Nico was no different. When we walked to the high street together, or met up at Forest Gate station, the world took on a slightly edgier rhythm. We would go to the supermarket next to the station and receive extra special attention from the security guard.

If Nico was staying with me, we would sometimes meet outside the supermarket in the high street. Despite having a list of sensible items to buy, somehow, we would almost always end up choosing a pizza. The phone shop in Woodgrange Road — where he got the screen for his phone repaired — is now gone, as part of the big refurbishment of the town centre. The gym he attended — set back off the road, near the weekly organic farmers market — is still there.

Nico — just over six feet tall, a barely contained ball of energy. I found out that he weighed twelve stone when they read out the coroner's report in court during the second trial. Tall, lean, muscular and handsome. Like many teenagers, his life is memorialized in images, from the banal and everyday to the spectacular. I will leave a single image here. It is one of the last photos that I took of him; he is standing in my living room. I had to take several to make sure that he looked his best and that his biceps were well defined. On his right hand, his tattoo is just about visible, it says "20??"

Figure 9: Nico Ramsay, in Forest Gate, January 2016

For days I couldn't write anything. Not a word. Not a single word. On the 17th February 2016, they turned off his life support. The medical staff had done everything they could.

Every test had been carried out, every possible medical intervention had been attempted. Five days of trying, five days of crying. And then he was gone.

***

On 17th February 2016, Nico died, five days after being stabbed. Those of us that were closest to him died a little also, and try as we might nothing will ever be the same. Everybody dies in the end. So, in many ways, grief is commonplace, everyday and mundane. Almost everyone will be living with grief, at some point and in some way. I'm building up to telling you about my grief. I'm getting there. It has taken me three years to write this. I write a lot. Every day. From carefully crafted words to send out into the world, to scribbled thoughts that are just for me. I write on paper, I speak notes into my phone, I make notes in my head. Random pieces turn up when I least expect it; reminders, warnings, pauses, songs of love and loss.

My family is large, we "roll deep", as they say. Intergenerational, intra-generational, too many to mention, Jamaican with additions of Greek, English, Irish, Ugandan, Ghanaian — need I go on? We are the classic post-war Commonwealth migrant story. My parents came to London in the 1950s. You've heard it all before: "no Blacks, no Irish, no dogs", monkey chants and the National Front. But they persevered. As the youngest in an immigrant family of five children, I absorbed the mantra that we were in a better place. We had a better life. We had more opportunity. Despite the everyday racism that put most of us out of school before time, that put us into contact with the police and the criminal justice system from early on, we kept on going.

We did all the things we weren't supposed to do. Teenage parents stayed together and became lifelong partners.

Early school leavers became graduates and postgraduates, working in the whitest places as teachers, chefs, and black taxi drivers. No matter what shit came our way, individually and institutionally, we kept going. And we believed, I believed, our love and familial ties would conquer all. Even when they locked us up, even when they sent us mad, I thought we would go on. Because we looked out for each other and had each other's back, I thought we could survive it all.

This chapter is my love song for Nico, my youngest nephew, the boy I named Essian (sixth son). The boy who had leukaemia as a child and grew up into a strong, caring and loving young man. A young man who was just getting ready, just starting to live, because had already lost so many years to illness.

13th February 2016 – 17th February 2016

Here are the briefest of details about how Nico died. I keep them brief because what I have learned is that people behave in ghoulish ways, even if they do not mean to. Insisting on more information, demanding to know what happened, sometimes blunt and direct, at other times wrapped up in a false air of concern. On the 13th February 2016, Nico was set upon by three assailants. They hit him, he fell to the ground, and they stabbed him in the heart. No explanation was given. All three were tried for murder. All three are serving life sentences.

Nico passed away at 18:26 on the 17th February, shortly after his life support was turned off.

The First Phone Call

"Come now, Mum! Nico's been stabbed." I was working in Finsbury Park when I got the call from my daughter.

I drove my ancient Ford Fiesta from Finsbury Park to the hospital. I was the first to arrive there, before the ambulance, transporting Nico, that was making its way at breakneck speed from the other hospital, nearer to the scene. I remember talking to a friend on the phone while I waited, chatting about some inconsequential nonsense, but not much more than that. I waited by the ambulance bay, anticipating his arrival.

Hospital: 1

I should have gone back to the hospital. I should have been there when they turned off the life support machines. I should have watched him journey on to the next place. But I couldn't bear it. I knew he had already gone, I saw him when the ambulance arrived and I saw when they carried him out. I saw that life had left him. He was grey and floppy, but I called out his name anyway. No response. No matter, I had hope. The paramedics ran into the hospital building at lightning speed, holding the mask over his face. I waited with the others for him to come out of surgery. What seemed like hours later, that first announcement, they got his heart started again. I hoped and I kept on hoping all through the next days that he would recover. Hope was not enough.

Try to imagine this. I saw my sister in the hallway, I think it was on day one, we had just met with the medical team, the consultant was very blunt. "No hope", she said, he'd stopped breathing for too long, we begged them to try anyway. But picture this, I said, as we leaned against the window, "we have to be prepared to let him go. Even if they revive him, Nico won't be the same, he wouldn't want that for himself." I said those words and they have haunted me ever since. But I only said it because I saw him and I knew he was already gone. So I held these two conflicting thoughts in my head, wanting him to get better, to wake up, while at the same time knowing that he had already passed.

With all of that, how could I tell a mother to let her son go? How could I?

Hospital: 2

My last contact with Nico was on the 17th, he was still hooked up to all the machinery, he felt very warm to touch. Over the last few days, I had watched the nurses fill in the charts and put drops in his eyes. The priest had been and said the last rites. We all knew that we would meet with medical team on the morning of the 17th, for further update after more tests. The night before, I had taken them home with me, my daughter and one of Nico's brothers. We all spent the night at my house, not saying much, not sleeping much.

I travelled back to the hospital in the morning. We were called into the family room, and they told us that there was really, really, nothing more they could do. I witnessed who was in the room, there were many, just don't ask me who. I left the hospital after the meeting. Before I went home, I called my daughter, she was expecting my call. I let her know. She told his brother. Afterwards she told me that both of them had half walked, half ran through a quarter mile of Forest Gate streets, ran like when they children, ran to their nan's house, holding each other up as they went. Ran to Granny for comfort and in the hope that she could make it better. She could not make it better. Later on that day, his brother went back to hospital. I stayed at home and waited. Waited for someone to call me, to tell me it was over. Did someone call me when it was over? I don't recall, but I know I was with my daughter while we waited. I don't remember. It's too much.

Nico was surrounded by people who loved him when he passed, so he did not travel the last part of his journey alone. By all accounts, it was peaceful, once the machines were turned off, it did not take long. It was time to go.

Police

We wanted to know what was happening with the third suspect. Two had been arrested at the scene, one had got away. One senior officer's response to our question was, "we have other murders". Callous yes, but we are a Black family, so we have no feelings. We are working class, so we matter less. This is not an aberration. I sat through hours of meetings with the police. I gave a statement to them. I sat in the court for days on end interacting with them. Their attitude ranged from a casual disregard to an overwhelming need to investigate all of us.

We were a nuisance, an inconvenience, and we certainly weren't grateful enough for the work they put in. And if you think that statement is cold-blooded and uncaring, consider this. Seconds after Nico's life support had been switched off the police walked into the room with a body bag — because in their eyes, he was evidence. More indifference, when I was threatened with arrest for failing to sign my name in the visitors' book. I had already written it numerous times over several days. I had seen the same officer more than once, but the rules are the rules, and non-compliance may get you locked up. According to him, Nico's hospital room was a crime scene. When I pointed out he was someone's child and not just a crime scene, that was sufficient for him to show his power. Black lives are always subject to control and surveillance, and even when near death, brutality and violence ripples under the surface.

In the Wake

After Nico passed away, I spent a lot of time at my sister's house. Marking time, doing chores, keeping busy, helping with the plans. Planning a funeral for a teenager, who does that? How do you come back from that?

I remember the first time that I got pulled up, literally pulled up by my collar, by some invisible hand. In the days and weeks that followed, I was at my sister's house, sitting in a chair in the kitchen, trying to avoid the endless stream of visitors. People just turned up, they tapped on the door, they came in and sat down. They left flowers and cards, they brought food and alcohol. People say "pay their respects", but I thought that once you did that you left. But most of them didn't, they stayed. Or came back the next day, and the day after that. I found a quiet-ish spot in the kitchen, near the fridge. One day my sister said that one of her sons has sent something for me to listen to. She picked up her phone, scrolled down, found the file and passed it over to me. The first few seconds made me crumple into my seat, I felt wounded, I heard Nico's voice on the song that his brother had recorded and I was folding. That's when I felt it the first time, an urgent tug at the back of my neck, pulling me upwards, forcing me to sit up straight. I started to listen again, and this time got past the first few seconds, then the next. It unnerves me to this day, I struggle to listen to it. While he raps, I can hear when his voice cracks, I can hear when the tears almost beat him. Later on, the music video brings it home even more. I see a group of desperately sad, broken individuals, trying to make sense of something senseless.[7] They are all too young to be in mourning. Mourning what exactly? What is? What might have been?

Another Caribbean tradition is the "nine night", when people gather together so that the spirit of the dead person should pass through safely to the other side. It is the final day of celebration of the person's life. I sabotaged my attendance. Why would I want to celebrate the end of Nico's life, when it had barely started? I went out for a meeting, and then for a drink. I got drunk, came home and went to bed. I woke up a few hours later to dozens of missed calls and messages. I had to go. I got there, very late, but I got there.

Someone, a man who scarcely knew Nico, announced that he would make a speech. He saw himself as an elder and, unasked and uninvited, this man took it upon himself to lead us in a prayer. He barely knew Nico, so he pronounced his name wrong, over and over again. Other people called out the correct pronunciation, but he carried on misspeaking with confidence. At first I winced, then I was angry, not just mildly angry but a boiling rage for those (and there are many) that make the tragedy of a young man's murder into an opportunity for self-promotion. As I did not trust myself not to say anything, I left the room.

31st March 2016

I am getting ready for the funeral on sunny spring morning. The service is at 1pm. My daughter is with me at my house, together we go through the motions of getting ready. I am trying not to cry, because if I start I may not be able to stop. When we are getting ready as individuals, or as a pair, there is always music. She puts on the first track, it's Frank Ocean. When it gets to the chorus we are in different rooms, we start to sing at the same time. In the chorus, Frank is imploring us to "kick off our shoes, and swim good". Swim where?, I'm thinking, none of this makes sense. None of this makes any fucking sense. Today, we bury a child, legally, technically a man because he was nineteen, but a young man who'd lived barely any of his adult life.

We locate our clothes, a white suit for me, and white jeans and a white shirt for her. I choose something else to listen to. It's Popcaan — a Jamaican dancehall artist. I used to hear Nico play this song when he stayed with me. I have heard it so many times, but today when Popcaan says "RIP to a loved one", I feel it again, that sharp tug at the back of my neck.

So we get ready, my daughter and me slowly, deliberately. Knowing that we have to do it. I'm dragging my feet. I don't want to go. I don't want to witness the finality of it all. I know he's gone but I don't want to know. It's time to go.

Funeral

Nico's body has been at his parents' house for a few days before the funeral. It is not unusual in Caribbean families to bring the body home. There are memories before this, but they are too painful to write and I don't have the words. Except that we watch as they bring the coffin outside of the house, and put it carefully, gently, on the hearse. The horses are very still and though a crowd has formed outside the house, there is silence. It is so quiet, then I hear it, choked back sobs that are getting louder. I wonder who is making all that noise. Then I realise, it's me. I have spent the last six weeks containing my sorrow and rage, and now it seeps out, and spills over.

Another memory, I'm in the church, standing in the pulpit to give the eulogy, I look down and see his brothers there, all five of them sitting in a row. I almost lose my nerve. When I look up I realise how many people there are. I've heard the phrase "a sea of faces" hundreds of times, but it really is a sea, of white fabric and blurred edges, with splashes of colour here and there. In my grief, I recognise no one else.

During the wake, on the day of the funeral, we show a series of films on loop. Nico at different stages of his life. I have seen it before, I already know the content of the individual films. There is the one where he plays his recorder. Another, where he sings nursery rhymes to his niece to comfort her when she is upset. I had seen them before but not like this, surrounded by people who missed him also. It is final, and I know he died, but I still expect him to walk through the door today.

Attending a funeral for a teenager, who does that? How do you come back from that?

At the end of the day, a smaller group of us gather at Nico's parents' house. Family and close friends, trying to speak about something that is unspeakable, trying to come to terms with the finality of it all. Some of the mourners (because on that day, that is who we were) are gathered in the street. The police arrive in two vans, and want to question the young men because more than three are gathered, and they are wearing the same colour clothes — white for the funeral. For the police, wearing the same colour implies "gang-related". So even today, of all the days, the police cannot leave us alone.

Taking Care

Constantly sorting the wheat from the chaff, to distinguish between those that come to help or offer a kind word and those who are looking for news. "What happened? What are the police doing? Have they caught them yet?" And what of the unspoken judgement, even from those who "mean well": that could never be my child, that could never happen to one of mine. Well, I'll leave that to your conscience. If you don't get it, I have neither the time nor the patience to explain it to you. For those that want to look beyond the headlines, I hope you can see what without a doubt, is that a nineteen-year-old young man lost his life. No, had his life violently taken.

Even now, it's still too distressing to speak of it. After three years, I still struggle to articulate it. When people talk about or mention knife crime, in my everyday life, in my academic life, on social media, I don't have the words to say what happened to him. It is always already on the tip of my tongue, it goes so far and then it stops. The words don't come. It's too much, the words are too heavy, and the aftermath, what happens in the wake of uttering those words. It means that I have to acknowledge again that he's gone, that his blood was let, and his life was dragged and kicked out of him. It is so monstrous, and so much, that I cannot bear to speak of how it makes me feel.

I often think about the young people that knew him, and how they manage the loss and the grief. I watched as young people in their teens and their twenties dig up the earth to shovel into Nico's grave, I saw them lay flowers and pour libation. Every time I hear Myers' song "Home", it resonates with me for that reason. He talks about not being able to forget that "you've seen your boy dead".

A telephone call and a six-month wait for counselling is the support that is on offer, even for those with the most traumatised lives. If, with all my years of life experience, I struggle to make sense of what happened, wrestle and resist feelings of anger, helplessness, sadness and rage, then what do you do with those feelings if you are a young adult? The thoughts of what might have been, and what I should have done, took my sleep for a long, long time. Out there, among us, are the walking wounded, dealing in some way with such deep levels of trauma.

***

One night, a few months after Nico died, I was walking home. I heard the sounds of a small party coming from one of the houses, I could hear people laughing and talking. Two years before, that would have been us; our family occasions were joyous, carefree and in the moment. We are much more guarded now. At any moment the joy could turn to pain, the laughter to tears. It can catch you like that, take you unawares and leave you gasping for breath. It is grief that makes me anxious in small spaces. I struggle to sit in a car, I have to drive it, or be the only passenger. The back seat of any vehicle is totally out of bounds, because being so enclosed sends me into a total panic. The tube is a challenge most of the time, so I navigate long, circuitous routes to get to where I need to be. It took years to work out, but I know why now. It was watching his coffin being lowered into the ground. It was watching, and taking part in covering Nico with the rich, heavy earth. Even now when I think about it, I feel suffocated, as though I'm drowning.

Last Words

Somehow, Nico, we go through life without you. A life that, no matter how hard we try, will never be the same. So here are my last words for you, my last song for you, the words I wish I had the chance to say fully while we were still on the same plane.

I remember you as small boy with almond-shaped eyes and a thick head of hair. The hair that changed colour and texture after so many rounds of chemotherapy. I remember the infectious smile, and the love for family and music. When you were about fourteen or fifteen, I recorded a video of you being interviewed for a young people's project. You are wearing your school uniform, a short-sleeved red polo shirt. As you sit at the desk, you seem comfortable, at ease. The interviewers ask you questions. This is what you have to say:

I'm Nico Ramsay, I go to Cumberland School and I live in Plaistow. I enjoy music, that's it really. I don't really watch TV but I like *Waterloo Road* and *EastEnders*. My favourite American artist, that would be Meek Mill, and for the UK, that would be Benny Banks.

When the interviewer asks you for three things that you would do to change the world, you say: "Stop Kony and stop all the children suffering in the world".[8] One of the final questions was about what you wanted to do when you were older, and your response: "I don't even know really, you know".

Sometimes I wonder if you knew that your time here was short; you were so ill for so long. I cannot imagine how you processed that experience. Maybe that's why you were so fearless. That terrible tattoo on your hand, I thought the writing said 2011, it was so badly drawn, but now I can see that they are question marks. Did you know?

At every step, the police investigation, the trials, I wanted to tell you what was going on, and then I remembered.

But if the dead really do talk, then I have listened, I heard you, I paid attention.

It has taken me a while to write down what I have heard. Too many emotions to sort through and the ongoing process of trying to come to terms with what happened to you, and the fact that you are no longer with us. I know that you can feel the love that we all had for you, but this is a personal message, from my heart to yours. I feel honoured to have known you. You came with a message that I should have taken more notice of. When you tried to cram everything in, living life to its absolute fullest, I told you to slow down, that you had all the time in the world. Maybe what I saw as the impatience of youth was something much deeper and more urgent. It is for the best to live in the now. I was wrong, and you were right; there is no point waiting for the perfect moment. I feel your presence in my heart and in my house. Your trainers are still under the bed. I would give anything to hear those size 9s rolling up the stairs. You, trying to be quiet and failing. I miss your laugh, your smile, and your unbounded good nature. We had some laughs here, some very good times, and when it was difficult, we sorted it out and got through it. We promised each other — no harsh words. I promised I would always be here for you and that will never change. That's why I went to the court, it's why I sat in all those meetings with the police, to support your mum, but also to take note and bear witness.

Near the end, you told the passer-by who was holding you, waiting with you until the ambulance arrived. You told them who had done this. You named your killers. I know now that death is not the end, it is a transformation of matter into another time, and onto another plane.[9] When I least expect it, I discover traces of you. I have told your story, Nico, some aspects of it at least. I hope I have done it well.

CHAPTER SEVEN
SOUNDING IT OUT

As I started to write this book, the 2018 World Cup was coming to an end. For a few days at least, London had a different energy. The sun shone, blazed in fact. Colonial and postcolonial migration histories meant that, for the first time in almost three decades, there was a real possibility of an England football team in the World Cup Final.[1] The troublesome trope of being "not from here" and sneering comments on social media about "cultural enrichment" whenever some crime is committed by "foreigners" abated somewhat. But beneath the celebrations, there were the usual cracks and tensions.[2] Manchester City footballer Raheem Sterling was still subject to negative stories in the media as well as vile racist abuse on the pitch. A Twitter thread from May 2018 outlines the most common narratives, arguing that Sterling demonstrates the worst aspects of Premier League football — he is cast as a "footie idiot" who is both "greedy" and "showy".[3] For Black youth, stories like these send a clear message — that holding on to a sense of belonging in this landscape is partial and contingent.

Taking C. Wright Mills' concept of the "sociological imagination" as a starting point, it is clear that in order to understand individual life we need to look at the society that individual lives operate in.[4] Using a sociological imagination allows us to understand how the broader landscape impacts upon the wins and the losses in contemporary Black lives. What I have tried to document here is how young Black lives matter in a society where inequality, exclusion and violence are normative. Exploring those private issues and public concerns in more detail, I set my sights on a particular area, the London Borough of Newham. I featured a specific place, Forest Gate, and then took the analysis to the level of the street, using a framework of hyper-local demarcation to hone in on life in one square mile.

When we look at the map, we can see there is a train station, a pub, a high street, coffee shops and a market that form the hub of the proposed urban village. We need to look at how people use those spaces, during the day, in the evening. What does life look like in this hyper-local area? It is clear that, for many, Forest Gate is a great place to live, with open green space, creative and cultural pursuits and "affordable" housing. But there are a number of variables such as age, housing tenure, ethnicity, and income that affect and challenge living in Forest Gate as a newly gentrified area.

Using a framework of hyper-local demarcation, we can look at how legislation, communities, sonic landscapes, and town planning come together to shape the lives of young people in the specific area of Forest Gate. Making use of public order legislation, ASBOs, dispersal orders, and public space orders allows the police and criminal justice system to further contain the movements and activities of young people in this area. Youth used to be a time to make mistakes, but on the whole those errors did not define you. Life could continue, with the past behind and not fixed in an identity of "ex-offender". National policy introduced the Criminal Records Bureau and then the Disclosure and Barring Service to protect children and vulnerable adults by checking the offending histories of potential employees. An unintended consequence, however, is that DBS checks are broadly applied. They are used as a checking process for further and higher education applications, housing, and insurance, as well as a wide variety of jobs, including retail (where most of the new jobs are).[5] For those from well-resourced WOW communities, it is entirely possible to come back from a criminal record or even a custodial sentence. For those from marginalised communities, even a relatively minor youthful misdemeanor can lock someone out of education and the world of work. Furthermore, immigration legislation means that coming into contact with the criminal justice system may result in deportation — even if you were born in the UK.

Neoliberalism, Austerity and Meritocracy

Neoliberalism, which centres the role of free markets and marks a shift away from state intervention in the wellbeing of its citizens, is now common sense. Young people who have grown up in the UK over the last forty years have known no other way to be. Post-war political consensus about a safety net for citizens is a distant memory for many. Hyper individualism and operating in the mode of survival of the fittest is the order of the day. The global financial crisis of 2008 highlighted the repercussions of savage, predatory capitalism for the many in terms of precarious employment, static incomes and an ever widening gap between rich and poor. The austerity programme, introduced as a UK government response to the global financial crisis, has amplified the effects of an unequal society. The effect of cuts to youth services were far reaching — a Commons Select Committee on youth violence found that across the country, youth services lost "£967 million in real terms". Councils spent less on youth justice and youth services, and between 2012 and 2016 more than six hundred youth centres closed.[6] The committee also highlighted that the lack of services was a contributing factor to the vulnerability of children and young people, particularly in the inner city. After taking evidence from a number of sources, the committee suggested that in terms of youth violence, England is in a state of emergency. They linked disadvantage and poverty to Organised Criminal Gangs' (OCG) ability to bring children and young people into their fold.

The Alston Report by the UN was damning with regards to the levels of poverty in the UK that had been exacerbated by the austerity agenda.[7] One key point that the report made was the disconnect between those who make and implement policy and those on the receiving end. However, rather than address the issues raised, the Conservative government's response was to threaten legal action. Despite evidence to the contrary, there is a stubborn refusal by the government to accept that large numbers of people live in poverty in the UK. According to them, if people work hard, they will do well. Meritocracy, the idea that people rise through hard work and talent, goes hand in hand with neoliberalism. According to Jo Littler, meritocracy acts as a means to legitimise contemporary capitalist culture.[8] In other words, it allows us to ignore social immobility and how intergenerational wealth offers socio-economic advantage. In a meritocratic age, all that matters is how hard you work, and how you market yourself. Matters of race, class and gender are not obstacles to individual success. Littler goes on to argue that in this landscape of competitive self-interest, some, inevitably, will get left behind. It is not an even playing field — rising to the top is more difficult for some, it depends on the availability of material and psychological resources.[9] A good education does not guarantee a well-paid job. Black Caribbean graduates, for example, continue to have lower than average earnings.[10]

Outsourcing of public services is deemed to be more efficient, but it often means poor service in health, welfare, housing, and education. As the same large companies dominate, they are deemed too big to fail so the inadequate service continues. Story after story reveals crises in health, care, and social provision, but these companies continue to be awarded contracts. The message it sends to those on the receiving end is that some people and organisations get away with it because they are powerful and have friends in the right places.

Newham, Transformed

In many ways, Newham is an exemplar of the UK's multicultural story. It has worked through its overt expressions of racism to become a municipality where 103 languages are spoken, and cultural diversity is now a cause for celebration.[11] Forest Gate, the focus of this book, started out as a relatively wealthy suburb in the Victorian era, until, like most of Newham, it fell into economic and social decline. For decades, Black communities experienced overt racism on the street and in the workplace, and institutional racism from the police. Black communities organised and campaigned against violence and injustice. In Newham, voluntary grassroots organisations such as the Newham Monitoring Project, The Renewal Programme,[12] and the East London Black Women's Organisation (ELBWO)[13] provided a wide range of community services, including training, support for refugees, childcare, advocacy, Saturday schools, and afterschool clubs.

In four decades, Newham has transformed itself to become a gentrifier's dream, where even the residual marks of far-right street politics have been erased. The Olympic Park site in Stratford will include a culture and education district, the V&A will have a new museum at Stratford Waterfront,[14] and UCL are building a new campus on the site.[15]

Newham has become one of the most multicultural boroughs in the country, and my focus has been on those young people with an Afrodiasporic (Black Caribbean, Black African) heritage. Despite regeneration, Newham at its core remains an impoverished place, an area of disadvantage and inequality. Those differences in life chances and opportunities have become even more marked with the recent wave of gentrification. All over London's inner city, house prices and rents are rising, but salaries and income have remained the same. Areas which were previously undesirable are now in demand by those that can afford it. Inner east London areas, such as Hackney, Shoreditch and Stoke Newington, felt this first. Now Newham is on the rise. Stratford station has been expanded and links easily to not only to the rest of the country, but Europe as well. Crossrail is coming, which will further reduce travel time as well as increasing access to central London. Forest Gate has a development plan that aims to turn it into an urban village, a desire that is repeated in many localities across London. The urban village will have a particular feel and will house unproblematic residents causing less drain on council finances.

So, for some residents, Newham really is a great place to live, despite the level of crime, and despite the heightened "gang activity". If you are able to inhabit the Well Off Worker or WOW community, then it is possible to cushion yourself from the ills that befall the area. With this in mind, it is entirely feasible to create an urban village in a multicultural area that not only contains bordered territories, but also pockets of whiteness.

But what of the young Black residents in this area? Life for them is different, and difficult. For them, it is often an offence to take up space in the city,[16] to have lives that are sociable and connected. They are often on the receiving end of policies designed to make the area a better place — there are fewer opportunities to gather on street corners, and the housing estates that provided room for play and creativity have been redesignated as "Badlands", places to be watched and controlled. Systems and institutions, housing policies, MAPPA orders, and the gang matrix work together to control behaviour at home and on the street.[17] In Newham, the police make frequent use of Section 60 legislation to stop and search young people as they move through public space.[18]

On the small housing estates, built on former bomb-damaged sites in Forest Gate, a sense of community was formed — often as a buffer against institutional and personal racial violence. Right to buy legislation changed that as residents sold up (after the mandatory three years) and moved out. Many former right to buy properties are now in the hands of private landlords. Housing tenure, for many, is precarious. Housing stock, for many, is of poor quality. Newham continues to have a high number of Houses of Multiple Occupation. Changes in Housing Benefit provision, and long waiting lists for social housing, also prompted a shift in population, to less expensive areas further afield.

Yet these same housing estates, street corners and youth centres contributed to the creation of an urban multiculture — among the young at least. The convivial endeavours of predominantly Black working-class youth meant that grime music could emerge from east London, with Newham as a primary site. After their parents and grandparents brought reggae and dancehall from the Caribbean, Black British youth adapted it to make something of their own. I explore this process in some depth in other work.[19] In young Afrodiasporic communities, grime and rap music provide a powerful sense of place and a compelling sense of belonging. In both the lyrics and the visual representations, young people express how life is for them. Music acts as ethnography, art and literature. It also provides a historical and contemporary engagement with place. However, for some young people, the opportunity to make music has been constrained by the town planning initiatives, policies and legislation that have been put in place to improve the area.

The three serious firearms incidents in Forest Gate that I discuss in Chapter Five are examples of what it means to live in a state of terror. Violence can come from anywhere and anyone. When an incident occurs, and the police come to investigate, the investigation process contributes to the violence, often rendering victims as criminals. Police and criminal justice processes bring further anguish to those already traumatised, to those already wary and weary of these interactions.

Newham may have pockets of gentrification, but it is still a poor borough. Serious crime, including gun crime, has increased. Police activity on the street has in many ways reverted to the highly militarised approach of the 1980s. Any event that relates to Black youth commands a heavy response and requires a show of force. For this group, policing is not done by consent. A warm and connected approach to the newer communities through personal contact and via social media heralds a change in policing style, for some. For others, aggressive policing simply forms part of a hostile environment that began soon after the post second world war commonwealth migration, and was amplified by David Cameron and Theresa May from 2010. In this climate, careful use is made of legislation enacted to counter terrorism, protect the environment, and maintain public order to place Black lives under surveillance. In Newham, legislation, development plans and the broad application of the gang matrix limits friendships and associations, thereby creating small lives and docile bodies.[20] For young Black lives this means that, although they operate in a highly mediated world with global networked connections, actual, real life connections are risky and problematic.

What we have here in this crucible of austerity, racist ideology, a hostile environment and poverty, is anguish, trauma and grief. So many people are living in social isolation while working through loss. So many young people have watched their peers lowered into a hole in the ground, have witnessed their friends removed, incarcerated or deported. So many young people are walking wounded, bearing all that trauma, all that distress, with little to catch it. The bereaved, the traumatised and the grief-stricken are supposed to somehow just carry on, and keep it moving. Politicians and policymakers operate at a distance, and these everyday issues do not touch them, as they are the concerns of the poor.

What I hoped to do with this book was provide context for those communities who dwell in the eye of the storm. As a way to begin to make sense of where we are and why it is like this, so that the Class of '91 — the four young people at the heart of why I wrote this book — know that they are not broken, the system is. People die at the hands of the state and we do nothing, children are murdered on our streets and we do nothing bar hold an inquiry, or create more institutions. All of this is possible because, for those in power and those with resources, life goes on. For some, life is a well-resourced cocoon of costly and exclusionary tastes, of craft beers, vegan haggis and artisan bread. As access to social life is mainly through consumption, most people in poor areas, like those who occupy these Forest Gate streets, are locked out of pleasurable, communal life experiences. Accessibility and acceptance of leisure and consumption choices highlights the value placed on different sectors of the community.

Gentrification as it occurs in Forest Gate throws these losses into sharp relief. Collective forgetting allows us to ignore the symbolic, structural and slow violence that occurs in young Black lives as they seek employment, pursue leisure interests and try to step into adult, independent life. In places like Newham, for young people like my Class of '91, daring to think about the future is a revolutionary act. In places like Newham, young lives are lost and damaged through violence and poverty. In 2016, I knew two young men who died. One I'd known his whole life, the other I met briefly. What we know of grief is that what is lost is more than the life itself. It is the promise of what might have been. The families that have to go on with an empty space. Not every mother who has lost a child to murder is weeping on the television. Somewhere, off camera, unseen, a million tiny heartbreaks occur, daily, weekly, by the minute. Hearts and RIPs posted on social media tell only part of the story. A story that is repeated over and over again, often in silence. Black deaths are normative and unless some mitigating factor is at play, even the most serious events raise local attention only. Somehow though, young Black lives go beyond survival mode, although they have become familiar with living with and through danger.[21] Black being, in the wake, offers a form of flourishing, and provides a way for musicians, recording artists, performers, and their audiences to hold out against a rendering and representation of Black lives that implies they have no value.[22]

Sounding It Out

In stories that relate to young Black lives, what is often foregrounded is failure, deficit and lack. The assertion by David Cameron that young Black men "are more likely to be in prison than at a top university"[23] prompted an inquiry, the Lammy Review.[24] A particularly problematic narrative of "aspiring rappers", or more recently the "roadman" trope, is often assigned to young Black men. Young Black women are rendered in different but equally damaging ways, as "angry" and "aggressive". Very rarely are young Black adults presented as vulnerable or in need of society's protection. Post-industrial Britain is committed to a neoliberal agenda as if there is no other way. Young citizens try to create a stable foundation out of zero-hour and fixed-term contracts in a gig economy that has outsourced mundane everyday tasks such as delivering food and collecting dry cleaning. Coupled with a weak welfare state and social ties that have become frayed by relocation and dispersal, young Black lives in the inner city exist in a state of advanced marginality.[25] At the same time, what is presented online and in educational dogma is that anyone can make it, they just have to work hard enough. But in this neoliberal landscape, only a few achieve the requisite levels of success.

In "Picture Me", south London rapper Dave lays out the conflicts and challenges of inner-city life, "going down the wrong road talking loads about goals and riches", and questions the fate of youths who do not become athletes or rappers.[26] What is promised is that the way to become independent, to live a life that is safe, fulfilling and secure is through hard work and a good education. And yet, according to the OECD, one in four graduates in England are underemployed, working in jobs which do not require a degree. In addition, they suggest that as many as 50% of graduates will never earn enough to pay back their student loan.[27]

On his track "Good Morning Britain", grime MC Chip works through his thoughts on a widely reported statistic that in 2018, London had a higher murder rate than New York.[28] This statistic fed into a narrative for more police, more police powers, and increased stop and search. In reality, the murder rate reached its peak in 2003 (when 204 people were killed). Since then, the rate has been decreasing.[29] Reflecting on the death of a teenage girl in a drive-by shooting, Chip wonders "when is change gonna come?". He makes a similar point to the UN Rapporteur Philip Alston, in that those that make the rules are far removed from those that live in poor areas. From the outside, people hear Tottenham (an area in north London) and think of the Premier League football team. But for Chip, Tottenham, his hometown, is replete with pain, and an increasing immunity to the everyday anguish that people have around them.

Looking back over the last forty years, we can see that competition and market forces have been positioned as the answer to matters of inequality and injustice. Individual solutions and individual responses ought to provide a safety net for societal issues. Food banks, charities and voluntary organisations are doing the work of the state for a fraction of the price. Scandals and failures dog private-sector delivery of public services, but ideological agendas allow them to stay in business.

Those who watch from the boundary get a partial, arm's length view. What I hope I have done here is look over the line, from up close. I have unmasked that what appears from afar to be a nihilistic approach to life is often a response to inequality and traumatic lived experiences. Hidden in plain sight, young people are yearning for a better world. A world that has possibility and hope, one where it is possible to be safe and secure. A world that has promise as well as menace.

In some ways, despite its well documented difficulties, online activity offers a counter to this, an alternative site for sociality. Young people share their optimism through political commentary, via music videos and lyrics, blogs, and social media. Podcasts allow commentary and discussion on topics that matter to them. Through aesthetic production and co-production of music and other creative events, young people from marginalised communities are carving out space to talk, engage and be free (even if that freedom is often framed in neoliberal, competitive terms). These are spaces in which knowledge is formed and communities are shaped.

In this book I've proposed a framework of "hyper-local demarcation" that allows us to consider the distribution of power and resources, as well as racialised narratives of economics, at the level of the street. I have shown how these techniques are at work through leisure pursuits and consumption patterns. In some measure, what I have written here may be unique to Forest Gate or Newham, other aspects may not be, as rising inequality affects quality of life in affluent societies across the global north. Community cohesiveness generates positive social relations, and without it the rise in anti-social behaviour, violent crime, and poor mental health continues. According to Pickett and Wilkinson, in more unequal societies people are less likely to, or be willing to, help each other, violence rises, and people become more in fear of each other.[30] Forty years of neoliberalism on either side of the Atlantic have embedded nihilistic, consumerist values as the only way to move society forward. In the United States, while income inequality is at its highest level since 1967,[31] the wealthy continue to enjoy a growth in income that surpasses those in the working- or even middle-class bracket. Simmering below the surface of luxury new builds and technological advance, the ever widening gap between rich and poor, the haves and have nots, is revealed via the sonic landscape, rising levels of violence and increasingly punitive measures to contain it. Pressures on emotional well-being are enhanced by precarious employment and an ineffective safety net for those who fall on hard times. What we see in affluent but unequal societies is a cycle of punitive measures, surveillance and control.

There is little doubt that young Black lives are lived with and through levels of disadvantage. Although life chances for Black youth from poor communities like Newham *are* impaired, we need to move away from looking at young Black lives as sites of negation and deficit, only considering what they lack as we view from the boundary. Instead, we must consider and address the structural constraints, taking a historical and contemporary view as we analyse how processes and techniques of racialised discrimination are at work.

Final Thoughts: A Better Place

We seem to be at a point where youth violence has become an industry. One recently advertised conference charged participants £25 per ticket and offered businesses sponsorship opportunities for anything between £250 and £4,500.[32] Events like these provide platforms to talk about the issues, and it may look as though something is being done.

But we already know what needs fixing, and we already know what to do about it. In a response to a question from the Serious Violence Select Committee, staff members from Project Future, a community organisation, described the interventions that they offered in their local area and explained why they did so. Based in the London borough of Haringey, this organisation works with young people aged mainly between eleven and twenty-five, but will also work with those who are older. They recognise that young people who come into contact with the criminal justice system need productive or meaningful activities to engage in, that often they have unmet mental health and wellbeing needs, and that their family lives are not always stable. They work in partnership to provide mental health services, employment, education and training and stability. We cannot arrest, medicate or imprison our way out of the challenges that face young Black lives in the inner city. And yet, as unelected UK Prime Minister Boris Johnson came to power, he immediately promised the recruitment of 20,000 more police officers and an increase in stop and search.[33]

But maybe a municipal shift against the worst effects of austerity is starting to happen. Newham is rebuilding its youth service provision, recruiting additional workers and increasing the sessions on offer across the Borough.[34]

Late capitalism is savage, and for many a combination of low wages, insecure work and little social protection means that it does not work. It therefore makes sense to do something radical to remedy the situation. In the UK, race and class add further layers of disadvantage in an already unequal society. The cost of marginality is too high to leave the problems unfixed, but local organisations spend time bidding for government funding so that they can deal with issues that they know exist. This is time that could be better spent working on the challenges that exist. Imagine how much could be done if these groups were simply allocated the resources and money that they need instead.

In past times, young people were seen as the future, whereas now they are framed as snowflakes for seeking affordable housing and secure employment and are derided for wanting work that does not damage their emotional wellbeing. Many young people start their adult life burdened by student debt that will probably never be repaid.

The lack of secure housing remains a fundamental matter. It would be relatively straightforward to provide young adults with homes at an affordable rent. Instead, millions are being pumped into a "Help to Buy" scheme that benefits only those on good incomes, or with access to intergenerational wealth.[35] Community organisations all over London know that young people need places to go and positive things to do. If London spent £43 million on a Garden Bridge across the Thames that was never built,[36] it must be possible to reinvest in publicly provided, accessible mental health services. The UK is the fifth richest country in the world. It has never been about a lack of finance, it has always been about the political will to allocate resources. We know what to do.

APPENDIX

In England and Wales the prison population numbers approximately 85,000, and continues to increase year on year. Prisoners from Black, Asian and ethnic minority communities are overrepresented.[1] The Ministry of Justice holds records on those serving a custodial sentence, as well those held on remand while awaiting trial. The criminal justice system in England and Wales also has the power to impose community orders — sometimes called community payback, these orders are for adults (often first time offenders) who have been sentenced for crimes such as assault or criminal damage.

Community orders and supervision orders, for those on suspended sentences where the sentence is delayed for a probationary period, are dealt with by the Probation Service. Probation services were within the remit of the Ministry of Justice. In 2014, the National Probation Service was part privatised. Those deemed to be low risk offenders (about 70% of those convicted) were moved to private companies under the Transforming Rehabilitation agenda[2].

In August 2018, I submitted two Freedom of Information requests to the Ministry of Justice. Appendix 1 details the number of Newham residents that were in custody at that time. The data in Appendix 2 relates to the "high risk" offenders who are being supervised by the Probation Service. In response to the Freedom of Information request, the MOJ could not provide figures for the "low risk" offenders supervised in the private sector.

Appendix 1. Freedom of Information Request: Custody

Ministry
of Justice

Disclosure Team
Ministry of Justice
102 Petty France
London
SW1H 9AJ

data.access@justice.gsi.gov.uk

20 August 2018

Dr Joy White

███████████████████████████████

Dear Dr White,

Freedom of Information Act (FOIA) Requests – 180812004

Thank you for your letter received on 10 August in which you asked for the following information from the Ministry of Justice (MoJ):

Your request has been handled under the FOIA 2000.

I can confirm that the MoJ holds the information that you have requested.

As at 30 June 2018, there were **786** individuals held in prisons, young offender institutions and immigration removal centres in England and Wales for which Her Majesty's Prison and Probation Service is responsible, with an origin address in the local authority area of Newham, as defined by our mapping software.

As postcode boundaries do not align directly with the local authority boundaries this data includes some individuals from postcodes not listed in your original question and does not include all individuals from the postcodes provided. The data are therefore representative of those with an origin address in Newham and not necessarily all those in postcode areas E6; E7; E12; E13; E15; E16.

Around 97% of prisoners have an origin location; i.e. addresses that are recorded in our central IT system. If no address is given, an offender's committal court address is used as a proxy for the area in which they are resident. This information is included in the data provided in the tables above. Those with no recorded origin are typically foreign nationals or those recently received into custody. No address has been recorded and no court information is available for around 3% of all offenders.

The numerical information provided has been drawn from administrative IT systems, which as with any large scale recording system are subject to possible error with data entry and processing. Further guidance on the considerations for processing a request under FOIA, can be found by following the links: http://www.legislation.gov.uk/ukpga/2000/36/contents and http://www.justice.gov.uk/guidance/foi-step-by-step.htm

Appeal Rights

If you are not satisfied with this response you have the right to request an internal review by responding in writing to one of the addresses below within two months of the date of this response.

data.access@justice.gsi.gov.uk

Disclosure Team, Ministry of Justice, 10.38, 102 Petty France, London SW1H 9AJ.

You do have the right to ask the Information Commissioner's Office (ICO) to investigate any aspect of your complaint. However, please note that the ICO is likely to expect internal complaints procedures to have been exhausted before beginning their investigation.

Yours sincerely

Prison Estate Transformation Programme
Her Majesty's Prison and Probation Service

2

Appendix 2. Freedom of Information Request: Probation

Ministry
of Justice

Disclosure Team
Ministry of Justice
102 Petty France
London
SW1H 9AJ

Dr Joy White

data.access@justice.gov.uk

4 September 2018

Dear Dr White,

Freedom of Information Act (FOIA) Request – 180821015

Thank you for your request received on 21 August in which you asked for the following information from the Ministry of Justice (MoJ):

Your request has been handled under the FOIA.

I confirm the MoJ holds information that you have requested, in relation to offenders managed by the National Probation Service (NPS) and it is provided to you in the table below.

	Total	Number of individuals in the community
Total	**1026**	**454**
Age		
18-21	99	44
22-25	184	73
26-35	372	159
35+	371	178
Gender		
Male	992	438
Female	34	16
Ethnicity		
Asian	229	112
Black	390	164
Mixed	56	22
Other	32	18
Not stated	57	15
White	262	173

The table shows the number of offenders under supervision by the NPS in the London Borough of Newham at the time your request was submitted. It is not limited to the postcodes specified in your request. The first column covers all offenders under probation supervision whose usual address is in Newham, including both those who are currently in custody and those in the community. The second column covers only those in the community. The table does not include offenders supervised by the London Community Rehabilitation Company, as the Ministry of Justice does not hold that data.

Appeal Rights

If you are not satisfied with this response you have the right to request an internal review by responding in writing to one of the addresses below within two months of the date of this response.

data.access@justice.gov.uk

Disclosure Team, Ministry of Justice, 10.38, 102 Petty France, London, SW1H 9AJ

You do have the right to ask the Information Commissioner's Office (ICO) to investigate any aspect of your complaint. However, please note that the ICO is likely to expect internal complaints procedures to have been exhausted before beginning their investigation.

Yours sincerely,

HMPPS Briefing and Correspondence Team

NOTES

Prologue

1   Littler, J. *Against Meritocracy* (Routledge, 2017).

2   Morton, S. "Killing of Corey Junior Davis in Forest Gate to Feature on Crimewatch", *Newham Recorder*, 2018. Available at: https://www.newhamrecorder.co.uk/news/crime-court/corey-junior-davis-shooting-crimewatch-appeal-1-5547613

3   King, J. (2017) "Man Suffers 'Life-Changing' Injuries after Forest Gate Shooting", *Newham Recorder*, 2017. Available at: https://www.newhamrecorder.co.uk/news/crime-court/man-suffers-life-changing-injuries-after-forest-gate-shooting-1-4964103

4   Mills, C. W. and Gitlin, T. *Sociological Imagination* (Oxford University Press, 2000), pg. 3

5   Sharpe, C. *In the Wake: On Blackness and Being* (Duke University Press, 2016)

Chapter One: Newham: Past and Present

1   According to Jon Burnett, over one hundred incidents of racial violence were reported in the immediate aftermath of the Brexit referendum (Burnett, J. "Racial violence and the Brexit state", *Race and Class*, 2017, 58(4), pp. 85–97). Claudio Schilter indicates that incidents had increased in areas perceived to have a high immigrant population (Schilter, C. "Hate Crime after the Brexit Vote: Heterogeneity Analysis based on a Universal Treatment." London School of Economics, 2017, p. 71).

2   According to the data, Newham has a population of 347,000. It is the most ethnically diverse borough, and the youngest, in the UK. Newham is ranked 8 out of 152 local authorities in England — rank 1 is the most deprived. It has the lowest life

expectancy, the highest level of TB, and the highest level of heart disease in all of the London boroughs. The unemployment rate is 5.7%; those who are economically inactive (unable to look for or take up work because of ill health, or caring responsibilities) is at 27%. The average weekly pay — £634 for men and £520 for women — before deductions is below the London average. The most common crimes in the area for the period from May 2018 to April 2019 were: anti-social behaviour: 24.17 per thousand population; violence and sexual offences have been combined: 28.82 https://www.newham.info/.

3   Booth, C. *Life and Labour of the People in London, Vol. 1* (Forgotten Books, 2012)

4   Eade, J. *Placing London: From Imperial City to Global City* (Berghahn, 2000)

5   A quick glance at the occupations of the Forest Lane residents in Forest Gate show: Robert Miller Physician & Surgeon at 128; Arthur William Shields, microscope maker at 139; and Martin J. Hosking, professor of music at 141.

6   Booth, *Life and Labour of the People in London*, p. 16

7   Eade, *Placing London*, p. 127

8   https://www.gracesguide.co.uk/West_India_Docks. The West India Docks closed to commercial traffic in 1980 and the Canary Wharf financial district was built on the site http://www.pla.co.uk/Port-Trade/History-of-the-Port-of-London-pre-1908

9   Adi, H. "London, Slavery and Abolition", *BBC News*, 2007. Available at: http://www.bbc.co.uk/london/content/articles/2007/03/23/abolition_hakim_adi_feature.shtml

10 The Coloured Men's Institute was founded in 1926 by Pastor Kamal A. Chunchie, as a response to the racial hostility that Black communities faced. The Institute offered food, clothing, and community activities (Visram, R. "Kamal A. Chunchie of the Coloured Men's Institute: The Man and the Legend", *Immigrants & Minorities*, 1999, 18(1), pp. 29–48).

11 A comprehensive history of the development of industry in West Ham can be found in: "West Ham: Industries", in *A History*

of the County of Essex: Volume 6, ed. W.R. Powell (London, 1973) pp. 76-89. *British History Online* http://www.british-history. ac.uk/vch/essex/vol6/pp76-89

12 Olusoga, D. *Black and British: A Forgotten History* (Main Market, 2017). p. 401

13 Elliot-Cooper, A. "When Did We Come to Britain? You Must Be Mistaken, Britain Came to Us", *Verso Blog*, 20 October 2015. Available at https://www.versobooks.com/blogs/2294-when-did-we-come-to-britain-you-must-be-mistaken-britain-came-to-us

14 https://humanzoos.net/?page_id=7002

15 Olusoga, *Black and British*, p. 451

16 Newham Monitoring Project, Newham: The Forging of a Black Community, Asian and Afro-Caribbean Struggles (Newham Monitoring Project/Campaign Against Racism and Facsism, 1991)

17 Ibid.

18 Patterson, S. *Dark Strangers: Sociological Study of the Absorption of a Recent West Indian Migrant Group in Brixton, South London*. Tavistock Publications, 1963.

19 As well as Enoch Powell's infamous 1968 "Rivers of Blood" speech, in the West Midlands in 1964 the Conservative candidate ran on a slogan "If you want a nigger for a neighbour, vote Labour". Also in June 1976, John Kingsley Read was charged with incitement to racial hatred after a speech on the steps of Stratford Town Hall https://discovery.nationalarchives. gov.uk/details/r/C11497258

20 See news reports at the time here, e.g. "1972: Expelled Ugandans arrive in UK", *BBC News*, 1972. Available at: http:// news.bbc.co.uk/onthisday/hi/dates/stories/september/18/ newsid_2522000/2522627.stm

21 https://www.theyworkforyou.com/debates/?id=1972-12-06a.1441.0.

22 Nigerian migration to the UK came after the end of Civil War in 1970, and mainly to take up higher education. A further wave

of economic decline and political tensions was the push behind another wave of Nigerian migration in the late 1980s (de Haas, H. "International Migration and National Development", 2006, p. 32). According to the Office for National Statistics, there are 190,000 Nigerian-born nationals living in the UK, https://www.ons.gov.uk/aboutus/transparencyandgovernance/freedomofinformationfoi/numberofnigerianslivingintheuk For Ghana, students and professionals travelled to the UK in the 1960s in search of higher education and then stayed on (Anarfi, J. and Kwankye, S. "Migration from and to Ghana: A Background Paper", 2003, p. 38).

23 A chart showing the number of asylum claims or other protection granted from the late 1980s until the present can be found here: https://researchbriefings.parliament.uk/ResearchBriefing/Summary/SN01403

24 "Migration to the UK: Asylum and Refugees", *The Migration Observatory*, 2019, https://migrationobservatory.ox.ac.uk/resources/briefings/migration-to-the-uk-asylum/

25 House of Commons Library Asylum Statistics: March 6 2019. Full Spreadsheet can be found here: CBP01403-Annex---dispersed-and-resettled-asylum-seekers-by-local-authority

26 https://www.newham.info/population/report/view/d19df39b53494c18a603cc355369e2ac/E05000483

27 http://bombsight.org/explore/greater-london/newham/

28 Newham Monitoring Project, *Newham*, p. 5

29 Ibid.

30 GB Historical GIS / University of Portsmouth, Newham District Through Time, Housing Statistics, Exclusive use of a bath, *A Vision of Britain through Time*. URL: http://www.visionofbritain.org.uk/unit/10064028/cube/HOUS_HAVE_BATH

31 GB Historical GIS / University of Portsmouth, Newham District Through Time, Housing Statistics, Housing Tenure, *A Vision of Britain through Time*. URL: http://www.visionofbritain.org.uk/unit/10064028/cube/HOUS_TENURE_GEN

32 Between 1951 and 1975, Newham lost forty thousand jobs. Several firms closed down or changed location (Ferguson, J. (2016) *The Newham Story: A Short History of Newham.* London Borough of Newham).

33 Ferguson, *The Newham Story*

34 Duman, A., Hancox, D., Minton, A. & James. M. *Regeneration Songs: Sounds of Investment and Loss in East London* (Repeater Books, 2018)

35 https://www.newham.gov.uk/Pages/News/Green-light-given-to-ambitious-300m-regeneration-plan-for-Royal-Docks.aspx

36 https://www.queenelizabetholympicpark.co.uk/our-story/transforming-east-london/east-works-jobs-skills-and-business-growth

37 Further details about the Crossrail/Elizabeth Line can be found here: https://tfl.gov.uk/travel-information/improvements-and-projects/elizabeth-line

38 Accountancy firm Grant Thornton created an index to measure the "vibrancy" of a particular area. There are six indicators, including prosperity, dynamism, and opportunity, inclusion and equality, and health, wellbeing and happiness. In 2018, out of 324 local areas, Newham ranked 312 (an improvement on the previous index where they ranked second from the bottom). More details can be found here: http://www.vibranteconomyindex.grantthornton.co.uk/?_ga=2.100676609.1092461290.1560054243-1369590599.1560054243#/england/newham

39 See https://www.newham.info/infographics/ for further information on Newham. See also http://newhamdata.wpengine.com/wp-content/uploads/2017/06/Forest-Gate-North-2011-UK-Census-profile.pdf for specific information on Forest Gate North. All data is drawn from 2011 census.

40 Newham Monitoring Project, *Newham*, p. 28

41 James, M. "Whiteness and Loss in Outer East London: Tracing the Collective Memories of Diaspora Space", *Ethnic and Racial Studies*, 2014, 37(4), pp. 652–667

42 Tompson, K. and Pilger, J. *Under Siege: Racism and Violence in Britain Today: Racial Violence in Britain* (Penguin, 1988); Newham Monitoring Project, *Newham*

43 Richardson, B. *Tell It Like It Is: How Our Schools Fail Black Children* (Bookmarks, 2007)

44 Newham Monitoring Project, *Newham*

45 Raines, H. "London Police Faulted as Racial Attacks Soar", *New York Times*, 24 March 1988. Available at: https://www.nytimes.com/1988/03/24/world/london-police-faulted-as-racial-attacks-soar.html

46 Newham Council Communications, *Newham's Legacy Story*, 2014, p. 4

47 (Furlong and Cartmel, 2007; Murray and Gayle, 2012; London Borough of Newham, 2017)

48 James, "Whiteness and Loss in Outer East London".

49 Ibid.

50 London Borough of Newham, *Newham's Local Development Framework: Supplementary Planning Document for Forest Gate*, 2010

51 See Newham Local Plan 2018 https://www.newham.gov.uk/Documents/Environment%20and%20planning/NewhamLocalPlan2018.pdf

52 London Borough of Newham, *Newham's Local Development Framework*, pg. 26

53 Bigga is a pseudonym.

Chapter Two: Neoliberal Times

1 Carrier, D. and Grierson, J. "Three Stabbed in Hyde Park as Water Fight Turns Violent", *Guardian*, 19 July 2016. Available at: http://www.theguardian.com/uk-news/2016/jul/19/stabbings-in-hyde-park-as-water-fight-turns-nasty

2 "Hundreds Join Black Lives Matter March through London", *BBC News*, 8 July 2016. Available at: http://www.bbc.co.uk/news/uk-england-london-36750533

3   *Regeneration Songs* explores, in some detail, the transformation of the London Borough of Newham as a site of investment and loss.

4   London Borough of Newham, *Newham's Local Development Framework*

5   Hall, S. "The Neo-Liberal Revolution", *Cultural Studies*, 2011, 25(6), pp. 705–728

6   Alston, P. "Report of the Special Rapporteur on Extreme Poverty and Human Rights on his mission to the United States of America", 2018. Available at: http://digitallibrary.un.org/record/1629536

7   Wall, T. "Firms Make Millions Out of 'By the Night' Flats for England's Homeless", Guardian, 26 May 2018. Available at: https://www.theguardian.com/society/2018/may/26/how-firms-make-millions-nightly-paid-temporary-flats-homeless

8   From the 1970s onwards, US and UK banks started to rely on computer-based systems for assessing credit risk. A fundamental problem of the highly globalised financial markets at the time of the US housing crisis was that many of the mortgage-backed debts turned out to be extremely "unhealthy", often referred to as toxic debts. The problem of the toxic debts, resulting from loans made to the subprime housing market, became more severe. The subprime market loaned money to people who could not afford to pay it back. As the scale of banking losses were announced, and, following the failure of leading investment banks like Lehman Brothers, banks were reluctant to lend to each other as they would normally do. The result was that banks were failing to fulfil a key banking function, namely to make loans and ensure the adequate flow of money into the economy (Steger, M.B. *Globalization: A Very Short Introduction* (Oxford University Press, 2017).

9   Lee and Wright (2011)

10 Hughes (2015)

11 Shildrick et al. (2010).

12 Hiam, L., Harrison, D., McKee, M. and Dorling, D. "Why is Life Expectancy in England and Wales 'Stalling'?", *Journal of Epidemiology and Community Health*, 2011, 72(5), pp. 404–408.

13 Eaton, G. "The Conservatives are in Crisis Over Austerity, Not Just Brexit", *New Statesman*, 2018. Available at: https://www.newstatesman.com/politics/economy/2018/08/conservatives-are-crisis-over-austerity-not-just-brexit

14 Chakrabortty, A. "These Councils Smashed Themselves to Bits. Who Will Pick Up the Pieces?", Guardian, 13 August 2018. Available at: https://www.theguardian.com/commentisfree/2018/aug/13/councils-austerity-outsourcing-northamptonshire-barnet; Sleator, L. "Councils Under Financial Strain", BBC News, 7 September 2019. Available at: https://www.bbc.com/news/uk-politics-45435368

15 The new legislation forces councils to offer all new tenants contracts of between two and five years. At the end of the fixed term, local authorities will have to carry out a review of the tenant's circumstance, and decide whether to grant a new tenancy, move the tenant into another more appropriate social rented property, or terminate the tenancy (Mason, R. "Council Tenants Lose Lifetime Right to Live in Property", *Guardian*, 9 December 2015. Available at: https://www.theguardian.com/society/2015/dec/09/council-tenants-lose-lifetime-right-to-live-in-property

16 Hall, "The Neo-Liberal Revolution"

17 An example here is the 1994 Public Order Act. Rave culture saw young people, fuelled by the new drug ecstasy, partying all night, often outdoors, or in unlicensed venues such as warehouses and aircraft hangars. To stay out of the clutches of the police, venues were shrouded in mystery, and only revealed via mobile telephone numbers. Following the "Summer of Love" in 1988, the Conservative government brought in the 1994 Criminal Justice and Public Order Act. It criminalised any large gathering featuring music with "sounds wholly or predominantly characterised by the emission of a succession

of repetitive beats". The new law also increased police powers to take non intimate samples such as hair, saliva, and mouth swabs. Samples did not need to be destroyed. (see Muncie, J. *Youth and Crime* (Sage, 2014))

18 (Thomas, 2018)

19 HMP Dovegate, HMP & YOI Doncaster, HMP Lowdham Grange, HMP Ashfield, HMP Thameside and HMP Kilmarnock.

20 Bulman, M. "More than 100 Women in Yarl's Wood Detention Centre Go on Hunger Strike Over 'Inhumane' Conditions", *Independent*, 2018. Available at: https://www.independent.co.uk/news/uk/home-news/yarls-wood-women-immigration-detention-centre-hunger-strike-home-office-a8223886.html

21 From 1997 until 2014, Serco had the franchise to run the Docklands Light Railway (DLR), which covers covers the City, Canary Wharf, and Stratford, and the south Newham area (Sharman, A. "Serco Loses Contract to Run Docklands Light Railway", *Financial Times*, 2014. Available at: https://www.ft.com/content/4adf2a26-0342-11e4-817f-00144feab7de). The full current range of services provided by Serco can be found here: www.serco.com.

22 https://www.serco.com/media/2551/speech-by-rupert-soames-to-the-british-services-association-june-2018.pdf

23 Rupert Soames is the brother of Nicholas Soames, the Conservative MP. His pay package included a £255,000 cash pension contribution. The pension payment was worth 30% of his £850,000 base salary. See https://www.thisismoney.co.uk/money/markets/article-6887301/Serco-faces-investors-ire-handing-boss-Rupert-Soames-255-000-pension-contribution.html

24 Further details of Serco salary scales can be found here: https://www.serco.com/uk/careers/prison-custody-officer-careers and here: https://career2.successfactors.eu//career?career_ns=job_listing&company=SercoGroup&navBarLevel=JOB_SEARCH&career_job_req_id=60746

25 Spice is a synthetic cannabinoid, designed to mimic the effects of cannabis. It was legal until 2016. It produces an intense high, and leaves users in a zombie-like state.

26 Sommerlad, J. "What is G4S and Why is it Dogged by Controversy?" *Independent*, 2018. Available at: https://www.independent.co.uk/news/uk/politics/g4s-hmp-birmingham-prison-private-security-contract-scandal-controversies-a8498956.html

27 Hattenstone, S. and Allison, E. "G4S Should Be a Failed Company by Now. But the Government Won't Allow It", *Guardian*, 23 December, 2016. Available at: https://www.theguardian.com/commentisfree/2016/dec/23/g4s-prisons-contracts-hmp-birmingham

28 "G4S Staff Sacked Over 'Teen Abuse'", *BBC News*, 12 January, 2016. Available at: https://www.bbc.com/news/uk-england-kent-35290582

29 Booth, R. and Hopkins, N. "Olympic Security Chaos: Depth of G4S Security Crisis Revealed", *Guardian*, 13 July 2012. Available at: https://www.theguardian.com/sport/2012/jul/12/london-2012-g4s-security-crisis

30 Travis, A. "G4S Admits Overcharging MOJ £24m on Electronic Tagging Contract", *Guardian*, 19 November 2013. Available at: https://www.theguardian.com/business/2013/nov/19/g4s-admits-overcharging-ministry-of-justice-tagging

31 Hattenstone and Allison, "G4S Should Be a Failed Company by Now. But the Government Won't Allow It"

32 Slater, T. "Gentrification of the City", in *The New Blackwell Companion to the City* (Blackwell, 2012)

33 Sibley, D. *Geographies of Exclusion: Society and Difference in the West* (Routledge, 1995)

34 London Borough of Newham, *Newham's Local Development Framework*

35 Irwin, S. "Lay Perceptions of Inequality and Social Structure", *Sociology*, 2018, 52(2), pp. 211–227.

36 Pickett, K. and Wilkinson, R. *The Spirit Level: Why Equality is Better for Everyone* (Penguin, 2010)

37 The Focus E15 Campaign has been in operation since 2013. A group of young mothers were served with eviction notices by their housing association after Newham Council cut their funding. When the women went to the council for rehousing, they were offered private rented accommodation in Manchester, Hastings, and Birmingham. As well as demands for more social housing, the group successfully campaigned to stop the demolition of a former council estate and refurbish it instead.

38 Phillips, D. and Pon, G. "Anti-Black Racism, Bio-Power, and Governmentality: Deconstructing the Suffering of Black Families Involved with Child Welfare", 2018, 28, p. 21

39 Fanon, F. *Concerning Violence*. (Penguin, 2008), p. 6

40 Ibid.

41 Nixon, R. *Slow Violence and the Environmentalism of the Poor* (Harvard University Press, 2011)

42 Graeber, D. "Dead Zones of the Imagination: On Violence, Bureaucracy, and Interpretive Labor: The Malinowski Memorial Lecture, 2006", *HAU: Journal of Ethnographic Theory*, 2012, 2(2), pp. 105–128.

43 Younge, G. and Barr, C. "Surge in Young Knife Deaths Amid Police Cuts and 'a Climate of Fear'", *Guardian*, 29 November 2018. Available at: https://www.theguardian.com/uk-news/2018/nov/29/surge-in-young-knife-deaths-amid-police-cuts-and-climate-of-fear

44 Wacquant, L. *Urban Outcasts: A Comparative Sociology of Advanced Marginality* (Polity, 2007)

45 Foucault, M. *Discipline and Punish: The Birth of the Prison* (Penguin, 1991)

46 Foucault, M. and Miskowiec, J. "Of Other Spaces", *Diacritics*, 1986, 16(1), pp. 22–27.

47 Sharpe, *In the Wake*

Chapter Three: Why Music Matters

1   J. Cole is a US rapper, singer and songwriter.

2   Gaza in this context refers to a long running feud in the reggae music industry. Fans either support *Gaza* — which refers to an area in Portmore Kingston, Jamaica — or *Gully* — also known as Cassava Piece, a proximate area in the same district. The areas are represented by two reggae artists Vybz Kartel for Gaza and Mavado for Gully. Both areas are garrison towns, and as such are often subject to violence (Dreisinger, 2010; Smith, 2010). (see Dreisinger, B. "Reggae's Civil War", *Village Voice*, 2010. Available at: http://www.villagevoice.com/music/reggaes-civil-war-6428428; Smith, L.B. (2010) *Jamaica Observer*. Available at: http://www.jamaicaobserver.com/columns/Lloyd-B-Jan-12_7320850)

3   Lyrics reproduced with the kind permission of Baseman: https://www.youtube.com/watch?v=-VAeFMUo0Qs

4   According to the Ministry of Housing, Communities and Local Government, there are 37 indicators of relative deprivation including: income, employment, health, education and skills, crime, barriers to housing and living environment. The Newham Info webpage provides further details on its impact. http://www.newham.info/factsandfigures

5   Farrugia, D. *Youth Homelessness in Late Modernity — Reflexive Identities* (Springer, 2016) Available at: http://www.springer.com/gp/book/9789812876843

6   My chapter in *Regeneration Songs* examines Newham's contribution to the grime scene in more detail.

7   Books that discuss the history of grime: Wiley, *Eskiboy* (Penguin, 2017); DJ Target, *Grime Kids: The Inside Story of a Global Grime Takeover* (Trapeze, 2018). Historical overview from Dan Hancox, *Inner City Pressure* (William Collins, 2018) and Jeffrey Boakye, *Hold Tight* (Influx, 2018). A photographic and narrative record is available from Hattie Collins and Olivia Rose in *This is Grime* (Hodder and Stoughton, 2016).

8   The "Black Atlantic" concept is a way to consider and analyse the creative expression produced predominantly by those from the Black diaspora. These cultural forms draw on, and are influenced by, the Caribbean, America and Africa.

9   Gilroy, P. *The Black Atlantic* (Verso, 1996)

10 Leyshon, A., Matless, D. and Revill, G. *The Place of Music* (Guilford Press, 1998)

11 See books about grime above.

12 Further detail can be found here: https://www.youtube.com/playlist?list=PLzVbXC_F7Oh_ZLDJ-zmZww0FOyBDsEZan

13 Lil Nasty, (2016) "Better Place (Plaistow)". Available at: https://www.youtube.com/watch?v=FMPJDwkqbwE

14 Baseman x Snizzy (2017), "Better Place (Forest Gate)". Available at: https://www.youtube.com/watch?v=-VAeFMUo0Qs.

15 Hudson, R. "Regions and Place: Music, Identity and Place", *Progress in Human Geography*, 2006, 30(5), pp. 626–634

16 The Jimi Hendrix Experience played the Uppercut on the afternoon of 26th December 1966 http://www.jimihendrix-lifelines.net/1966/styled-5/styled-13/index.html.   Stevie Wonder performed as a sixteen-year-old in October 1967 http://www.e7-nowandthen.org/2013/11/when-stevie-wonder-played-forest-gate.html.

17 Muncie, *Youth and Crime*, p. 250

18 If you are Black, contact with the criminal justice system often results in a criminal record (see White, J. *Urban Music and Entrepreneurship: Beats, Rhymes and Young People's Enterprise* (Routledge, 2016)). Contact can come via the police, or the local council in the case of an Anti-Social Behaviour Order (ASBO), now replaced by Civil Injunctions and Criminal Behaviour Orders. In London, in 2017/18, the Metropolitan Police carried out "3 stop and searches for every 1,000 White people, compared with 29 stop and searches for every 1,000 Black people" (see https://www.ethnicity-facts-figures.service.gov.uk/crime-justice-and-the-law/policing/stop-and-search/latest). In certain occupations (for example in the care and retail

sectors), criminal convictions are never spent, and always have to be declared. In other roles, a conviction is a real deterrent to securing employment. But the reach of the Rehabilitation of Offenders Act 1974 (ROA) goes beyond employment. Disclosure of a criminal record is required by educational institutions, insurers and housing providers. https://www.unlock.org.uk/policy-issues/specific-policy-issues/further-reform-to-the-roa/.

19 Minisparks, "Its ms – Promotional Hood Video", https://www.youtube.com/watch?v=LPhEAm3FoFM

20 London Borough of Newham, *Newham's Local Development Framework*

21 WoodGrange E7, "Who's That Click", https://www.youtube.com/watch?v=X5EJw033Ads

22 James, "Whiteness and Loss in Outer East London

23 Baseman and Snizzy, "Talks", https://www.youtube.com/watch?v=TM4urXhsPvU

24 James, "Whiteness and Loss in Outer East London", p. 11

25 Gilroy, P. "Between the Blues and the Blues Dance: Some Soundscapes of the Black Atlantic", in Bull, M. and Back, L. (eds.) *The Auditory Culture Reader* (Berg, 2003), p. 383

26 Sharpe, *In the Wake*

27 Ibid., p. 19

28 Hartman (2019)

29 According to Richard Bramwell and James Butterworth, who carried out field research in Newham in 2015, 75% of youth provision was cut. Bramwell and Butterworth looked at the role of institutions — youth centres — in supporting and shaping rap culture. They argue that the service provision at Forest Gate youth centre made a significant contribution to the vibrant rap culture in East London (see Bramwell, R. and Butterworth, J. "Beyond the Street: The Institutional Life of Rap", *Popular Music*, 2019. Available at: https://ora.ox.ac.uk/objects/uuid:f44969cb-ce07-4d0f-bc12-162796b88bea)

30 For young people from poor areas, EMA provided a much needed income stream for hobbies and leisure interests,

including music. It was scrapped in England in 2010 but continues in Scotland and Wales. EMA was income assessed, and paid directly to students from low income families.

31 London Borough of Newham, *Newham Local Plan 2018: A 15 Year Plan Looking Ahead to 2033* (2018), p. 48

32 London Borough of Newham, *Newham's Local Development Framework*

33 London Borough of Newham, *Newham Local Plan 2018*, p. 50

34 The SBTV Better Place is a series of fifteen videos on the theme of home. It features artists from London, Birmingham and Sheffield rapping about their area. Further detail can be found here: https://www.youtube.com/playlist?list=PLzVbXC_F7Oh_ ZLDJ-zmZww0FOyBDsEZan

35 Newham Council Communications, *Newham's Legacy Story*, p. 4

36 Ciaran Thapar writes extensively about UK Drill. This article highlights the moral panic against the genre. See: Thapar, C. "The Moral Panic Against UK Drill is Deeply Misguided", *Pitchfork*, 12 September 2018. Available at: https://pitchfork.com/thepitch/ the-moral-panic-against-uk-drill-is-deeply-misguided/

37 White, *Urban Music and Entrepreneurship*

38 Beauman, N. "Is Violence Holding Grime Back?", *Guardian*, 2006. Available at: http://www.theguardian.com/music/ musicblog/2006/nov/06/isviolenceholdinggrimeback; Jones, S. "Rap Music Feud Behind Gun Violence in Birmingham", *The Grime Report*, 2010. Available at: http://thegrimereport. blogspot.co.uk/2010/06/rap-music-feud-behind-gun-violence- in.html; Muggs, J. "Violent Grime on the Increase", *The Arts Desk*, 2013. Available at: http://www.theartsdesk.com/new- music/violent-grime-increase; Fatsis, L. "Policing The Beats: The Criminalisation of UK Drill And Grime Music by the London Metropolitan Police", *The Sociological Review*, 2019.

Chapter Four: Why Live Anywhere Else?

1 Farrell, S. "Community Venues Breathe Life unto the UK's Left Behind Areas", *Guardian*, 20 July 2018. Available at: https://

www.theguardian.com/business/2018/jul/20/community-venues-breathe-life-into-the-uks-left-behind-areas

2   Shaw, A. "Revealed: The 10 Most Crime-Ridden Streets in Newham", *Newham Recorder*, March 2018. Available at: https://www.newhamrecorder.co.uk/news/crime-court/revealed-the-10-most-crime-ridden-streets-in-newham-1-5434990

3   Tweet from Councillor Rachel Tripp 2:21 PM - 21 Apr 2018 https://twitter.com/rectripp/status/987667626959745026?s=03

4   Metropolitan Police Forest Gate North tweet at 3:34pm 21 May 2019 https://twitter.com/MPSForestGteNth/status/1130829248552460288

5   Acton, L. "Community Helps Raise Cash for Business Affected by Road Works", *Newham Recorder*, May 2019. Available at: https://www.newhamrecorder.co.uk/news/residents-rally-to-get-local-business-through-rough-spot-1-6075682

6   Gillet, F. "Forest Gate Estate Agents Portico Gutted in Fire after Car Ploughs into Shop Front", *Standard*, August 2017. Available at: https://www.standard.co.uk/news/london/forest-gate-estate-agents-portico-gutted-in-fire-after-car-ploughs-into-shop-front-a3616946.html

7   Jensen, O. and Gidley, B. "'They've Got Their Wine Bars, We've Got Our Pubs': Housing, Diversity and Community in Two South London Neighbourhoods", in Pastore, F. and Ponzo, I. (eds) *Inter-Group Relations and Migrant Integration in European Cities: Changing Neighbourhoods* (Springer, 2016), p. 224.

8   See News reports at the time here:
    In Uganda: http://news.bbc.co.uk/onthisday/hi/dates/stories/september/18/newsid_2522000/2522627.stm
    In Kenya: http://news.bbc.co.uk/onthisday/hi/dates/stories/february/4/newsid_2738000/2738629.stm

9   https://www.newham.info/population/

10 A chart showing the number of asylum claims or other protection granted from the late 1980s until the present can be found here: https://researchbriefings.parliament.uk/ResearchBriefing/Summary/SN01403

11 Rattansi, A. *Bauman and Contemporary Sociology: A Critical Analysis* (Manchester University Press, 2017) p. 9

12 Eighteen-year-old Sami Sidhom was killed yards from his door in April 2018. See: https://www.newhamrecorder.co.uk/news/clapton-cfc-ride-for-sami-sidhom-1-6022873

13 Gidley, B., Hanson, S. and Ali, S. *Identity, Belonging & Citizenship in Urban Britain* (2018) p. 9 Available at: https://www.gold.ac.uk/media/documents-by-section/departments/research-centres-and-units/research-centres/centre-for-urban-and-comm/CUCR_FINAL_REPORT.pdf

14 Ibid., p. 29

15 Lees, L. "Gentrification and Social Mixing: Towards an Inclusive Urban Renaissance?", *Urban Studies*, 2008, 45(12), pp. 2449–2470.

16 Shaw, K. "Gentrification: What It Is, Why It Is, and What Can Be Done about It", *Geography Compass*, 2(5), 2008, pp. 1697–1728.

17 Slater, "Gentrification of the City", p. 580

18 Hamnett, C., Ramsden, M. and Butler, T. "Social Background, Ethnicity, School Composition and Educational Attainment in East London", *Urban Studies*, 44 (7), 2007, pp. 1255–1280; Lees, "Gentrification and Social Mixing"; Harding, A. and Blokland, T. *Urban Theory* (Sage, 2014).

Chapter Five: Wins and Losses

1   I interviewed Paulette, a Black woman of Caribbean heritage, in 2019. I asked her: What was Forest Gate like in 1974? Paulette had moved from Holland Park in west London in the early 1970s, at the age of thirteen. She remembered the high street being quite vibrant with many different shops. She attended Forest Gate School, which is located in Forest Lane (see map). Paulette still lives and works in Newham, but in another part of the borough.

2   I spoke to Winston in 2019. I have used a pseudonym for him.

3   King, "Man Suffers 'Life-Changing' Injuries after Forest Gate Shooting"

4   Morton, "Killing of Corey Junior Davis in Forest Gate to Feature on Crimewatch ; Reporters, 2018)

5   At the time of writing, the inquest into Edson Da Costa's death had just opened, and was scheduled to run until 4th June 2019. Inquest — a charity that looks into state-related deaths — reported that "Black people had been significantly overrepresented in deaths following use of force by police". In 2018, there were twenty-three deaths in police custody, the highest for fourteen years. Of these deaths, eight were Black. https://www.inquest.org.uk/iopc-stats-2018

6   Townsend, M. "Four Black Men Die. Did Police Actions Play a Part?", *Observer*, 2 September 2017. Available at: https://www. theguardian.com/uk-news/2017/sep/03/four-black-men-die-police-restraint-no-officers-suspended-bryant-cumberbatch-charles-da-costa

7   "Forest Gate Clashes: Six Police Officers Injured in London Protest Over Man's Death after Traffic Stop", *Telegraph*, 26 June 2017. Available at: https://www.telegraph.co.uk/news/2017/06/25/protesters-clash-police-25-year-old-died-days-stopped-police/

8   Video footage can be seen here: https://www.channel4.com/news/police-injured-in-protests-following-edson-da-costa-death

9   Tompson and Pilger, *Under Siege*

10   Sivanandan, A. "From Resistance to Rebellion: Asian and Afro-Caribbean Struggles in Britain", *Race and Class*, 23(2–3), 1981, pp. 111–152, p. 131.

11   Margaret Thatcher was interviewed for *Granada TV* on 27th January 1978: https://www.margaretthatcher.org/document/103485

12   We can see here the beginnings of "political blackness" as a movement and as a strategy to challenge racism. In the Tomson book for example, which was written in 1988, the author states: "I should point out that the use of the word 'black' in the book refers

to all non-whites and thus includes Asian people and others affected by racism" (Tompson and Pilger, *Under Siege*, p. x).

13 Sivanandan, A. "From Resistance to Rebellion"

14 What came to be known as the "Rivers of Blood" speech was made on 20th April 1968. Enoch Powell, a Conservative MP, condemned Commonwealth immigration, and called for the repatriation of Black migrants. The speech proved to be both controversial and divisive. Powell was sacked from the Shadow Cabinet.

15 Sivanandan, A. "From Resistance to Rebellion", p. 124

16 The British Nationality Act 1981 came into force on 1st January 1983. It removed the rights of Commonwealth and Irish citizens to become British citizens by registration. Instead they were to be expected to apply for naturalisation if they wanted to acquire British citizenship. Anyone over the age of ten who applies for naturalisation or registration as a British Citizen is subject to the "good character test". In the most recent Home Office guidance, "good character" is not defined. Instead it invites an individual approach, based on a number of factors, including: criminality, international crime or terrorism, financial soundness (being in debt), notoriety (your standing and reputation in your local community), deception and dishonesty, immigration-related matters. The list is not exhaustive (Home Office, 01/19). As of March 2019, the cost to apply for naturalisation is £1,330, and for registration £1,206 (adult) and £1,012 (child). Indefinite Leave to Remain (ILR), allows permanent residency, and the freedom work or study, but no right to live in the UK. The cost to apply for ILR is £2,389. Figures are taken from https://www.gov.uk/government/publications/visa-regulations-revised-table/home-office-immigration-and-nationality-fees-29-march-2019. After a minimum of twelve months with ILR, you can apply for British citizenship — see costs above. In specific circumstances, ILR can be revoked https://assets.publishing.service.gov.uk/government/uploads/system/uploads/attachment_data/file/469493/Revocation_of_Indefinate_Leave_October.pdf.

17 The "Windrush generation" refers to approximately 500,000 people who came to the UK from Caribbean countries between 1948 and 1971. Although adults were granted Indefinite Leave to Remain (ILR) in 1971, many were children and had travelled on their parents' documents. In 2012, a further change to the law meant that without their own documents, this group of people could not continue to work, or access services. In some cases, people were deported because they could not prove that they had a right to stay in the UK.

18 Kapoor, N. and Narkowicz, K. "Unmaking Citizens: Passport Removals, Pre-Emptive Policing and the Reimagining of Colonial Governmentalities", *Ethnic and Racial Studies*, 42(16), 2018, pp. 45–62.

19 Ibid., p. 48

20 Ibid.

21 Tompson and Pilger, *Under Siege*, p. 21

22 The Police and Criminal Evidence Act 1984 (PACE) was introduced partly as a response to the difficulties caused by the use of "sus", as well as to high profile miscarriages of justice such as the Guildford 4 and the Birmingham 6. PACE was introduced on the recommendation of a Royal Commission on Criminal Procedure. It aimed to balance the rights of the individual against the powers of the police. It introduced audio recordings of interviews and set out codes of practice for stop and search, arrest, detention, investigation, identification, and interviewing detainees.

23 Rollo, J. "The Special Patrol Group", in *Policing the Police, Volume 2* (John Calder, 1980), p. 224.

24 Ibid.

25 In the subsequent inquiry, SPG officers who took part in the policing of the event were found to be in possession of unauthorised weapons (baseball bats, crowbars, hammers). In the official report, only released in 2010, it was thought that Peach's skull was probably crushed by an unauthorised weapon such as a cosh. See: https://www.met.police.uk/foi-ai/af/

accessing-information/met/investigation-into-the-death-of-blair-peach/

26 Hall, S., Roberts, B., Clarke, J., Jefferson, T. and Critcher, C. *Policing the Crisis: Mugging, the State, and Law and Order* (Macmillan, 1978)

27 One community response was the People's Day of Action in March 1981 — an eight-mile march from Deptford to Hyde Park in Central London.

28 Newham Monitoring Project, *Newham*, p. 50

29 The charges against Martin Newhouse were subsequently reduced to manslaughter. He received a sentence of four-and-a-half years.

30 See for example Newham Monitoring Project, The Renewal Programme https://www.renewalprogramme. org.uk/our-history, and the East London Black Women's Organisation (ELBWO): http://www.womensgrid.org.uk/ archive/2009/05/21/elbwo-east-london-black-womens-organisation/

31 http://www.gdrc.org/icm/partner-sys.html provides an overview of the "pardner" (or partner) as a popular system of micro-credit in the Caribbean — essentially a partnership to save collectively, with one trusted person acting as the "banker".

32 Tompson and Pilger, *Under Siege*

33 In 1964, Peter Griffiths, a Conservative, used that as his campaign slogan and won. Labour were expected to win the seat in Smethwick in Birmingham. See: https://www.bbc.co.uk/ historyofthebbc/memories/elections/smethwick

34 Richardson, B. *Tell It Like It Is*; Bryan, B., Dadzie, S. and Scafe, S. (2018*) Heart of the Race: Black Women's Lives in Britain* (Verso, 2018)

35 http://www.ukcensusdata.com/forest-gate-north-e05000483#sthash.HzuoGBN8.dpbs
http://www.ukcensusdata.com/forest-gate-south-e05000484#sthash.VHfx7NVA.dpbs

36 Stratford Shopping Mall has recorded up to one hundred rough sleepers each night. See: https://www.newhamrecorder.co.uk/

news/charity-boss-warns-homeless-crisis-in-newham-risks-becoming-a-serious-public-health-issue-1-5542278. A further recent increase is due to a nearby squatted site being cleared and boarded up. See: https://www.newhamrecorder.co.uk/news/features/recorder-letters-stratford-centre-derelict-pubs-and-get-fit-for-charity-1-6087920

37 https://www.ellcchoicehomes.org.uk/Data/ASPPages/1/1270.aspx

38 Shaw, A. "Revealed: The 10 Most Crime-Ridden Streets in Newham"

39 Willis, D. (2018) "Community Conversations", p. 26.

40 Burford, R. (2018) "Newham Had the Highest Number of Murders in London in the Last Year", *Newham Recorder*, 2018. Available at: https://www.newhamrecorder.co.uk/news/crime-court/newham-had-the-highest-number-of-murders-in-london-1-5764803 (Accessed: 6 November 2018).

41 Ibid.

42 Overview and Scrutiny Unit, *Report of the Crime and Disorder Scrutiny Commission into Youth Violence and Gang Crime in Newham* (London Borough of Newham, 2014)

43 In Tottenham, on 4th August 2011, Mark Duggan was shot dead by police. Protests soon turned to civil unrest, not only in London but also in other parts of the country.

44 In their review of the gangs matrix, Amnesty argue that "the Gangs Matrix is a database of suspected gang members in London... [It] purports to be a risk-management tool focused on preventing serious violence. But in practice it is a racially discriminatory system that stigmatises young black men". Trapped in the Matrix: Secrecy, stigma, and bias in the Met's Gangs Database, Amnesty UK, 2018

45 Amnesty UK, 2018

46 The data breach was reported in local and national news. Data included home addresses, dates of birth and the alleged associated gang of approximately 200 people. The leak was revealed during the Serious Case Review into the death of Corey

Davis. Newham Council was fined £145,000 by the Information Commissioners Office (ICO). https://www.newhamrecorder.co.uk/news/politics/council-fined-over-gang-matrix-leak-1-5980358

47 Cited in Muncie, *Youth and Crime*

48 Four young men were found guilty of possession of a firearm with intent to endanger life and conspiracy to commit GBH. They were aged between twenty-one and twenty-three years. Each one was handed a twenty-six-year sentence — twenty-three years plus three years on extended licence. See: https://www.independent.co.uk/news/uk/crime/clown-mask-drill-rapper-gang-lekan-akinsoji-jailed-e7-a8803506.html

49 Tompson and Pilger, *Under Siege*

Chapter Six: In Memoriam: Nico Essian Ramsay

1 https://www.historyextra.com/period/victorian/history-backgrounder-knife-crime-britain/ looks at how in the 1890s, young men from poor areas in England's major cities fought using belt buckles and knives. Acid attacks were a phenomenon in Victorian England deemed to be carried out by "irrational women", and then reported on again in a "gang" context in 2017. See https://legalhistorymiscellany.com/2017/09/13/acid-attacks-in-nineteenth-century-britain/

2 A Home Affairs Select Committee stated that serious youth violence was a "social emergency".

3 From 1993 until 2010, the prison population in England and Wales expanded, almost doubling from around 44,500 to almost 85,000 https://www.crimeandjustice.org.uk/resources/criminal-justice-times-austerity. Prisons in the UK are at capacity, with approximately 84,000 in custody (https://www.gov.uk/government/statistics/prison-population-figures-2019). England and Wales have the highest incarceration rate in Western Europe (https://www.theguardian.com/society/2017/mar/14/england-and-wales-has-highest-imprisonment-rate-in-western-europe). As of July 2019, there

are 812 children — aged 18 or under — in custody (https://www.gov.uk/government/statistics/youth-custody-data).

4 Metropolitan Police used "tactical contact" techniques on suspected stolen mopeds. Technique involved the police ramming vehicles into the suspects.

5 The research report, "Austerity and Health: The Impact in the UK and Europe", indicated that benefit cuts and sanctions increased homelessness and that homelessness increased the risk of "food insecurity, infectious diseases and physical harm". On reviewing literature from the EU and the USA, they noted that evidence suggests that poverty or economic hardship worsens mental health. Austerity is regressive, in other words it hits the poor hardest and widens social and economic inequality. See Stuckler, D., Reeves, A., Loopstra, R., Karanikolos, M. and McKee, M. (2017) "Austerity and Health: The Impact in the UK and Europe", *European Journal of Public Health*, 27(suppl_4), 2017, pp. 18–21.

6 Gary Younge's year-long study sought to challenge misconceptions about knife crime in the UK. The data suggests that "taken as a whole two thirds of young people killed by knives in Britain, including London, are not Black".
See: https://www.theguardian.com/membership/series/beyond-the-blade

7 Lil Nasty, Better Place (Plaistow) [Music Video]: SBTV https://www.youtube.com/watch?v=FMPJDwkqbwE

8 Stop Kony 2012 was an early viral Twitter and Facebook campaign. It related to a thirty-minute film that exposed the Lord's Resistance Army's use of child soldiers in east Africa. The film received over a hundred million views in six days. See Boulton, C. "In Defense of 'Slacktivism': How Kony 2012 Got the Whole World to Watch", in Coombs, D.S. and Collister, S. (eds.) *Debates for the Digital Age: The Good, the Bad, and the Ugly of Our Online World* (Praeger, 2015).

9 Sharpe, *In the Wake*

Chapter Seven: Sounding It Out

1   The 2018 England World Cup squad had twenty-three players
     and included ten with Caribbean and/or African heritage: Kieran
     Trippier, Kyle Walker, Jesse Lingard, Danny Welbeck, Marcus
     Rashford, Raheem Sterling, Ruben Loftus-Cheek, Dele Alli,
     Trent Alexander-Arnold and Danny Rose. For the first time since
     1990 England reached the semi-final of the tournament. Five of
     their starting players for the semi-final game were of Caribbean
     heritage, one of them — Raheem Sterling — was born in Jamaica.

2   Racism on and off the pitch has been a constant feature of the
     English football landscape. For a further exploration of cultural
     racism surrounding a previous football tournament, the 1996
     European Football Championship (Euro 96), see Carrington B.
     "Football's Coming Home' But Whose Home? and Do We Want
     It?: Nation, Football and the Politics of Exclusion" in Brown, A.
     (ed.), *Fanatics: Power, Identity and Fandom in Football* (Taylor and
     Francis, 2002). In the essays, Ben Carrington examines how the
     contemporary racism exhibited in Frank Skinner and David
     Baddiel's *Fantasy Football* television show was subtly coded as
     "laddishness" and banter, despite Baddiel using Blackface, and
     singling out one player — Jason Lee — for series-long ridicule.

3   Keyworth, A. "[Thread] a selection of times when our national
     press have chosen to run stories on Raheem Sterling. 1. The
     one where Raheem was "tired".pic.twitter.com/6K3cHu6r7T",
     @adamkeyworth, 28 May 2018. Available at: https://twitter.
     com/adamkeyworth/status/1001218545588502530?lang=en

4   Mills and Gitlin, *Sociological Imagination*

5   A recent report by *Unlock* carried out a survey on the impact of
     DBS checks on people from Black, Asian and ethnic minority
     backgrounds. Existing data showed that African and Caribbean
     people are over-criminalised and over represented at all
     levels of the criminal justice system. They found that "the
     overwhelming majority (79%) cited employment as one of the
     problems they faced. The other most common problems were

relationships (34%), volunteering (30%), insurance (26%), travel/immigration (23%) and college/university/education (23%)". See Stacey, C. "Double Discrimination: The Impact of Criminal Records on People from Black, Asian and Minority Ethnic Backgrounds", *Unlock*, 2019. Available at: https://www.unlock.org.uk/wp-content/uploads/Double-discrimination-Full-report-July-2019.pdf

6   Home Affairs Committee, *Serious Youth Violence*. Sixteenth Report of Session 2017–19, p. 61. Available at: https://publications.parliament.uk/pa/cm201719/cmselect/cmhaff/1016/1016.pdf

7   Alston, "Report of the Special Rapporteur on Extreme Poverty and Human Rights on his mission to the United States of America".

8   Littler, *Against Meritocracy*, p. 2

9   Ibid., p. 3

10   Data from 2019 showed that Black Caribbean graduates had lower than average earnings — £18,000 as opposed to an average of £19,900. See: https://www.ethnicity-facts-figures.service.gov.uk/education-skills-and-training/after-education/destinations-and-earnings-of-graduates-after-higher-education/latest

11   Aston Mansfield, *Newham — Key Statistics* (Aston Mansfield Charity, 2011).

12   Founded in 1971, the Renewal Programme aimed to "to work against racist attitudes, high unemployment and low educational achievement". Further details are available here: https://www.renewalprogramme.org.uk/our-history

13   ELBWO was founded in 1979. Its activities have scaled back but it still runs an after-school club in Forest Gate. See: http://www.womensgrid.org.uk/archive/2009/05/21/elbwo-east-london-black-womens-organisation/

14   The V&A East project will also include a research centre in partnership with the Smithsonian Institution. See: https://www.vam.ac.uk/info/va-east-project

15   This will be UCL's largest expansion since it was founded in 1826. See: https://www.ucl.ac.uk/ucl-east/]

16 "Wayward Lives, Beautiful Experiments: In Conversation with Saidiya Hartman", Backdoor Broadcasting Company, 31 May 2018. Available at: https://backdoorbroadcasting.net/2019/05/wayward-lives-beautiful-experiments-in-conversation-with-saidiya-hartman

17 White, J. "Controlling the Flow: How Urban Music Videos Allow Creative Scope and Permit Social Restriction", *YOUNG*, 2016.

18 Section 60 Criminal Justice and Public Order Act 1994 is a preventative measure. It gives police the right to search people in a defined area — it can be applied to a few streets, or the whole borough. Once a s.60 is in place, police officers do *not* need to have reasonable grounds to stop and search individuals. In a response to a question about the application of a borough-wide section 60: "Could you provide a list of all dates and times since 1 January 2011 during which a Section 60 PACE order issued by the Metropolitan Police has covered the area of a whole borough? Please also provide the borough name in each case": Newham 2017: 12 times, in 2018 22 times. The figures for neighbouring boroughs are: Hackney: 2017 -1, 2018 – 9; Redbridge: 2017 - none, 2018 - none; Waltham Forest: 2017 - 2, 2018 - 1 , and Tower Hamlets: 2017 - none, 2018 - 2. Figures for 2018 are to May 2018. https://www.london.gov.uk/questions/system/files/attachments/Batch%205%20-%20MQ2018_0972%20-%20Stop%20and%20Search%20section%2060%20%282%29_13.pdf

19 White, *Urban Music and Entrepreneurship*

20 White, J. "Controlling the Flow: How Urban Music Videos Allow Creative Scope and Permit Social Restriction", *YOUNG*, 25:4, 2016

21 Lorde, P.A. and Clarke, P.C. *Sister Outsider: Essays and Speeches* (Ten Speed Press, 2007)

22 Sharpe, *In the Wake*

23 Ross, T. "David Cameron: 'Black People More Likely to be in Prison than at a Top University'", *Telegraph*, 31 January 2016. Available   at: https://www.telegraph.co.uk/news/politics/

david-cameron/12131928/Labours-David-Lammy-to-lead-government-race-review.html (Accessed: 8 August 2019).

24 Despite making up just 14% of the population, BAME men and women make up 25% of prisoners, while over 40% of young people in custody are from BAME backgrounds. The Lammy Review was an independent analysis of the disproportionality regarding Black, Asian and minority ethnic individuals in the criminal justice system at the point of arrest onwards. See: https://assets. publishing.service.gov.uk/government/uploads/system/uploads/ attachment_data/file/643001/lammy-review-final-report.pdf

25 Wacquant, *Urban Outcasts*

26 Dave, "Picture Me", 2016 https://www.youtube.com/watch? v=lnI5scOpuYQ

27 OECD, *Education at a Glance 2018* (OECD Publishing, 2018). Available at: https://read.oecd-ilibrary.org/education/ education-at-a-glance-2018_eag-2018-en (Accessed: 2 August 2019).

28 Chip, "Good Morning Britain", 2018 https://www.youtube. com/watch?v=-4IKg3MueOY

29 Lee, G. "FactCheck: Is London Really Deadlier than New York?" *Channel 4 News*, 2019. Available at: https://www.channel4. com/news/factcheck/factcheck-is-london-really-deadlier-than-new-york

30 Pickett and Wilkinson, *The Spirit Level*

31 Picchi, A. "Income Inequality in America is at its Highest Level in More Than 50 Years", *CBS News*, 26 September 2019. Available at: https://www.cbsnews.com/news/income-inequality-in-america-is-at-its-highest-level-in-more-than-50-years-census-report-today-shows/

32 The conference was planned to take place in London in July 2019 and aimed to "collaborate with individuals and organisations to establish a comprehensive directory of contacts, programmes and resources that will enable communities to quickly identify and access support when needed".

33 Grierson, J. "Will PM's Police Hiring Spree Make Streets Safer?",
    Guardian, 2019. Available at: https://www.theguardian.com/
    uk-news/2019/jul/30/boris-johnson-promises-will-police-
    hiring-spree-make-streets-safer

34 London Borough of Newham, "Recruitment Now Underway for
    Biggest Expansion for a Generation in London's Youth Services",
    2019. Available at: https://www.newham.gov.uk/Pages/News/
    Recruitment-now-underway-for-biggest-expansion-for-a-
    generation-in-Londons-Youth-Services.aspx

35 Launched in 2013, the Help to Buy Scheme offers shared
    ownership and equity loans https://www.helptobuy.gov.uk/
    shared-ownership/. The National Audit Office indicated that
    most people who bought under the scheme could have afforded
    it anyway. See Partington, R. "Most Help-To-Buy Recipients
    Could Already Afford a Home", *Guardian*, 12 June 2019.
    Available at: https://www.theguardian.com/business/2019/
    jun/13/nao-says-60-of-help-to-buy-buyers-did-not-need-state-
    support

36 Walker, P. "Garden Bridge Charity Spent £53.5m with No
    Construction, TfL Finds", *Guardian*, 2019. Available at: https://
    www.theguardian.com/uk-news/2019/feb/13/garden-bridge-
    charity-spent-535m-with-no-construction-tfl-finds

Appendix

1   See the Lammy Review for details: https://assets.publishing.
    service.gov.uk/government/uploads/system/uploads/
    attachment_data/file/643001/lammy-review-final-report.pdf

2   Under the Transforming Rehabilitation agenda the MOJ
    dissolved 35 probation trusts and created Community
    Rehabilitation Companies (CRCs). By 2015, the private sector
    delivered the majority of CRC services. A review in April 2019
    found that CRC services "fell short of expectations with high
    rates of reoffending and poor value for money, so contracts
    would be terminated early." https://www.nao.org.uk/report/
    transforming-rehabilitation-progress-review/

ACKNOWLEDGMENTS

I thought about this book for a long time. I had started to write it many times, and then put it down because some parts were too painful. I didn't know how to get the words I had in my head into a form that I (or anyone else for that matter) could make sense of. When I knew what I wanted to do, weird as it was, and how I wanted to do it, the task was to find a publisher that understood that. I spent a lot of time thinking about who to approach, and then as I read through some of the other chapters in *Regeneration Songs* (where my chapter on the grime scene in Newham was published), the penny dropped. Repeater seemed to be a place for work that didn't quite fit a mould. Tariq Goddard immediately got what I was trying to do, so I have to thank him for that.

My Class of '91 deserve a special mention here for the frank discussions and snatched conversations that opened my eyes to the challenges of everyday living for young Black people in Newham.

Thank you to those who commented and encouraged along the way: Neil Adams, Lindsey Bourne, Andy Duke, Jonathan Ilan and Ebony Reid. Blossom Lewis, Yvonne Robinson, and Maxine Webster, read many of the chapters and accompanied me when I did my field research. I appreciate your time and your input into this work. A big thank you also goes out to my sister Dawn, who shared my family responsibilities so that I could write.

Thanks also to Paulette, Winston, and Bigga, the older heads that provided a captivating personal history of

Newham from forty years ago. Their stories, and others like them, that go un-noted and un-recorded, need their own platform before the narratives are erased or forgotten. I will do something lasting and positive with your words. Challenging as it may be, we owe it to the next generation to let them know what it was like to grow up in those times, and how we came to survive them.

Three more extra special mentions: my daughter Karis who read many of the chapters, including Chapter Six, the one that was the most difficult for me to write. Thank you, Karis, for putting aside your own sadness about Nico to sit with my words and read them with love and care. Also, when I had tried many times to contact Baseman for permission to use his lyrics for Chapter Three, Karis got on the case and made the necessary connection via Snapchat. Thank you, Baseman, for allowing me to use your words. Natalie Nzeyimana read early drafts and took the time to offer insightful and helpful comments along the way. Thank you, Natalie, for introducing me to the work of Christina Sharpe and Saidiya Hartman, and letting me know that both of these women were visiting London to talk about their work in person. Thank you to the ISRF (Independent Social Research Foundation) for funding a residential research week in 2017. It gave me time to really think about what I wanted to do.

And finally, a shout to all those who supported me along the way to get this book finished — almost on time. I appreciate you all.

Joy White

REPEATER BOOKS

is dedicated to the creation of a new reality. The landscape of twenty-first-century arts and letters is faded and inert, riven by fashionable cynicism, egotistical self-reference and a nostalgia for the recent past. Repeater intends to add its voice to those movements that wish to enter history and assert control over its currents, gathering together scattered and isolated voices with those who have already called for an escape from Capitalist Realism. Our desire is to publish in every sphere and genre, combining vigorous dissent and a pragmatic willingness to succeed where messianic abstraction and quiescent co-option have stalled: abstention is not an option: we are alive and we don't agree.